The Courage to Dream

Vincent Harding (1931–2014) was a central participant in the struggles of the American civil rights movement. A colleague and confidant of Martin Luther King, for whom he prepared several speeches, he drafted King's famous oration delivered at Riverside Church in 1967 condemning the Vietnam War. Professor of Theology from 1981 to 2004 at Iliff School of Theology in Denver, Colorado, he was also co-founder and chairperson of Veterans of Hope, an initiative emphasizing non-violent approaches to social change. His books include *There is a River: The Black Struggle for Freedom in America* and *Martin Luther King: The Inconvenient Hero*.

Daisaku Ikeda (1928–) was born in Tokyo, Japan, and lived through the devastation of World War II as a teenager, which left an indelible mark on his life. These experiences fuelled his lifelong quest and passion to work for peace and people's happiness, rooting out the fundamental causes of human conflict. In 1975, Ikeda became the first president of Soka Gakkai International, a Buddhist network that actively promotes peace, culture and education, whose members come from over 190 countries worldwide. He is the author of more than 100 books on Buddhist themes, and received the United Nations Peace Award in 1983.

Advance Praise for

The Courage to Dream

I have long known that Vincent Harding is the most profound living interpreter of the legacy of Martin Luther King Jr. His extended dialogue with internationally renowned Buddhist leader Daisaku Ikeda is packed with valuable insights about what Vincent calls the movement to 'expand democracy in America'. These two extraordinarily wise, generous, and compassionate intellectuals reveal their own backgrounds and experiences as they shed light on the contributions of major leaders such as King, Gandhi, and Obama, while also calling attention to the roles played by women and 'ordinary people' in social justice struggles. As Harding and Ikeda learn from each other, readers of this inspiring book can listen and be enlightened.

—Clayborne Carson, editor of the papers of Martin Luther King Jr, and founding director, the King Institute at Stanford University

This book is a true gift. It's a wonderful introduction to the spiritual values and moral commitments that animated the black freedom struggle, interwoven with brilliant reflections on the necessity of continuing the movement to expand and deepen our democracy.

It is difficult to imagine two people better suited to engage in and to encourage such a deep, probing dialogue about the work that is required to build a multi-racial, multi-ethnic democracy rooted in a shared awareness of the dignity and humanity of us all.

—Michelle Alexander, author, *The New Jim Crow*, and associate professor of law, Ohio State University

Vincent Harding is a national treasure, and his wisdom is profoundly nourishing in this national moment. He embodies the evolution of humanity and spirit that is possible in the context of American democracy. This groundbreaking dialogue with Daisaku Ikeda is a gift to all of us who approach American democracy not as something that is irreparably broken but which we have the privilege and pleasure to grow to new maturity.

—Krista Tippett, host of *On Being With Krista Tippett*, and author, *Einstein's God*

More than a dialogue between two important practitioners and thinkers of democracy, it is a touchstone for anyone who wants to advance the possibility of peace and democracy in the world. Anchored in the civil rights movement, Martin Luther King Jr, and Buddhism, the sixteen conversations offer insight into the core values that must inform the work of each individual engaged in the struggle for democracy. These conversations are also an affirmation of the essential role of everyday people and youth in advancing the possibility of democracy. Yet for me the enduring value of these conversations is how continuously and beautifully Daisaku Ikeda and Vincent Harding remind us of the power of hope and love . . . the essential guide to and source of renewal for anyone working to create a fair, just, and democratic world.

—Ceasar McDowell, professor of the practice of community development, MIT, and President, Interaction Institute for Social Change

The Courage to Dream

On Rights, Values and Freedom

VINCENT HARDING

AND

DAISAKU IKEDA

Published in 2016 by
I.B.Tauris & Co. Ltd
London • New York
www.ibtauris.com

ISBN: 978 1 78453 475 2
eISBN: 978 0 85772 973 6

A full CIP record for this book is available from the British Library

Printed and bound in Great Britain by T.J. International, Padstow, Cornwall

Contents

Daisaku Ikeda and Vincent Harding, Tokyo, 1996

O, yes, / I say it plain,
America never was America to me,
And yet I swear this oath—
America will be!
An ever-living seed, / Its dream
Lies deep in the heart of me.

Langston Hughes,
'Let America Be America Again', 1938

Preface

Daisaku Ikeda

'I Have a Dream' – a great dream for the future becomes a light of hope illuminating our lives. A dream for the triumph of justice becomes the driving force for progress, rallying the people. And a dream for the harmonious coexistence of all humankind becomes a bond of peace creating a new global society.

Professor Vincent Harding is a renowned historian and champion of human rights who stood alongside Dr Martin Luther King Jr, a key leader of the civil rights movement, in upholding a noble dream and devoting his life to its realization. I first met Professor Harding in Tokyo nearly twenty years ago, on 17 January 1994, Martin Luther King Jr Day. Throughout the years since Dr King was felled by an assassin's bullet, Professor Harding, as Dr King's spiritual comrade, has kept his legacy alive and continued his fight for equality and justice.

Professor Harding and I felt an immediate bond of empathy and understanding upon our initial meeting. I sensed in him the passion of a proud, steadfast champion of human rights and an unbending resolve to battle all forms of prejudice and inhumanity that threaten the dignity and worth of human life.

At that first meeting, Rosemarie Freeney Harding, Professor Harding's wife, stood by his side with a wise, lovely smile. Until her death in 2004, she was for many long decades his true, faithful comrade in the fight for justice, as well as a renowned peace and human rights activist in her own right.

Dr King gave his life to the struggle to eradicate racial discrimination, to establish equality in civil rights, to eliminate poverty and to resolutely oppose all forms of war and violence. At the same time, Dr King's thoughtful, impassioned gaze was focused on a more distant horizon for the future of human society: the establishment, as Professor Harding repeatedly refers to it in this dialogue, of the 'beloved community'. Dr King's ultimate goal, I believe, was to build beautiful, loving ties joining all the people of the world into a global family, transcending all differences, including race, religion, language and gender, while respecting our rich diversity.

In this dialogue, I speak of Bodhisattva Never Disparaging, a figure who appears in the important Mahayana Buddhist scripture the Lotus Sutra. Bodhisattva Never Disparaging embodies in his practice the spirit of unqualified faith in the dignity and worth of all beings – an absolute commitment to respect and revere them, no matter what the cost, even at the risk of his life. I believe that the 'beloved community' of which Professor Harding speaks is also a 'respectful community' as represented by Bodhisattva Never Disparaging: a community shining with respect for the dignity and worth of life.

Though Dr King is frequently referred to as a leader of the civil rights movement, Professor Harding believes that the term 'civil rights movement' is an inadequate description of the cause to which he and Dr King dedicated themselves; he suggests instead that it should be seen as a broader 'expansion of democracy'. Many individuals have devoted their blood, sweat and tears to this movement to expand democracy. We must never forget these unidentified champions, nor the fact that this movement itself is never-ending. It is an ongoing effort, to be passed from one generation to the next, from adults to youth, for all eternity.

This expansion of democracy is not just a matter of changing government policies or something that can be achieved by a select group of political leaders. It can only be accomplished when every individual in society, awakening to their own dignity and worth as well as that of others, stands up to join hands with their fellow citizens to build a better world based on true humanism.

1 January 2013 marked the 150th anniversary of President Abraham Lincoln's signing of the Emancipation Proclamation. 28 August of the same year is the fiftieth anniversary of Dr King's historic speech 'I Have a Dream' in front of the Lincoln Memorial in Washington, DC. The dream of which Dr King spoke with such passion and commitment is still alive today, and it continues to inspire those striving courageously, in the face of many obstacles and difficulties in this world of suffering, for peace and humanity.

As long as we still have this dream, hope remains eternal. No matter what tribulations arise, no matter what storms of adversity beset us, as long as there is hope, the great march forward of the people, the great river of justice, cannot be held back. We will flow magnificently onward with the stirring cry, 'We shall overcome!'

Dr King was shot and met the end of his precious life on 4 April 1968. I learned of this tragedy when I was in the midst of preparations for the first entrance ceremony of the Soka Junior and Senior High Schools,[1] which would take place in a few days; I was also laying the groundwork for the establishment of Soka University, which would occur three years later. I offered prayers of the deepest condolence.

In Dr King's book *Where Do We Go from Here: Chaos or Community?*, the Japanese edition of which was published immediately following his assassination, he asserted his unyielding conviction: 'One day we must come to see that peace is not merely a distant goal that we seek but a means by which we arrive at that goal. We must pursue peaceful ends through peaceful means.'[a]

The indispensable requirement for this kind of transformation is education – education that fosters a courageous spirit of non-violence within people's hearts. The people's movement for peace and humanity that the Soka Gakkai International is promoting is also an ongoing, never-ending struggle and its success or failure rests entirely on fostering youth to carry on the movement and its ideals. This is why I chose education as the crowning effort of my life and have devoted all my energies to it.

Today, forty-five years since Dr King's death, how much of his dream has become a reality? If he were alive today, what would he say about our world and the United States, and what actions would he take? These questions have been present in my thoughts as I engaged in this dialogue with Professor Harding.

We who live in the twenty-first century have a mission and a duty to study the great spiritual struggles of our predecessors and open a new path forward. As a participant in this dialogue, I will be deeply gratified if this book ignites a bright torch of courage and hope in the hearts of all those people of our world today – especially our youth, in whose dreams our future rests – who dedicate themselves to pressing courageously onward, shoulder to shoulder, for the sake of justice and peace.

Preface

Vincent Harding

Near the end of his thoughtful preface to this dialogue, President Ikeda makes a statement that is characteristic of the man and his vision, a statement that caught my attention and reminded me why I constantly found such pleasure in our long-distance conversation: 'We who live in the twenty-first century have a mission and a duty to study the great spiritual struggles of our predecessors and open a new path forward.' This urgent encouragement has been on my mind a number of times since our dialogue ended. (Will it really end, or will it continue in many manifestations for the rest of our lives?)

One important opportunity to respond to my brother Ikeda's challenge opened up even before we closed off this stage of our conversation. Not long ago, a group of men and women deeply involved in the twentieth-century human rights struggles of our country decided to bring ourselves together as a National Council of Elders.[1] One of our major reasons for coming together was to make available to a younger generation whatever we could share of our long experience in working for a 'more perfect Union'.[2]

Just as we were organizing the Elders, we learned that a new generation of young people was coming together, calling itself the

'Occupy movement' and focusing especially on the great and growing income inequities in America and the unjust political domination accompanying this. What we Elders discovered was that the young Occupy organizers were eager to talk with us, to share experiences, to learn and to teach.

In a sense, we have engaged in serious dialogue with our children, and we Elders are glad to see that members of the Occupy generation have now volunteered their time and resources to assist fellow citizens who suffered great personal and property losses in our recent storm on the East Coast.[3]

Of course, the most prominent of our children was not in the Occupy movement but in the White House. Remembering some of the dialogue President Ikeda and I shared about the possibilities that Mr Barack Obama represented for America and for the world – and feeling a real sense of connection to this young man in my role as an Elder and as a carrier of the African-American portion of his story – I have paid close attention to him.

In the course of his first term, I reminded myself and others that it is essential for us to believe that 'We the People' have great responsibilities in a democracy. And occasionally, I wrote to my nephew/brother/son in the White House. Recently, I wrote to encourage him in a difficult time, the time after his re-election, a period of great financial and political difficulty. As I often do, I reminded my adopted son of the powerful words he had spoken some time before: 'We did not come to fear the future. We came here to shape it.'[4] When he is at his best, I believe that my nephew/son really believes these words and wants to live them out with us. So, I wrote to him:

> Do not be afraid, my son. Do not be afraid to speak the names of the poor, to shape a new future with them, and with all this diverse, beautiful, and motley crew that is coming to make up our nation again. I think that's what our most progressive eighteenth-century 'founder' Tom

> Paine meant when he said, 'We have the power to begin the world over again.' I'm sure that's what our beautiful brother Martin Luther King Jr meant when he kept calling at the end, 'America, you must be born again.'

I don't know whether my brother/son/nephew Obama has seen any of my letters. But I do believe that this is the direction my brother Ikeda was pointing to when he urged me and all of us to 'open a new path forward'.

Let's go.

CONVERSATION ONE

A More Perfect Union

IKEDA: I am honoured to participate in this dialogue[1] with such a great champion of human rights, compassionate educator and pre-eminent American scholar of social history. I look forward to exploring with you the focal issues of the twenty-first century – the issues of human rights, peace and education.

You were a trusted friend, colleague and ally of Dr Martin Luther King Jr, both of you taking part in the civil rights movement. In our dialogue, I hope that you will share your anecdotes and memories of Dr King as you discuss at length, for the sake of young people, the philosophy of faith and action that was forged and tempered in your struggles for human rights. I also want to contemplate and explore together what we must do – what path humanity must take – to create a peaceful global society.

HARDING: This dialogue gives me the chance to reminisce about Dr King's life as well as engage in some autobiographical reflection. Words cannot express my appreciation for this opportunity. My daughter and friends all strongly encouraged me to participate in this dialogue.

IKEDA: Let's have a free, wide-ranging discussion. Dr King once said, 'An individual has not started living until he can rise above the narrow confines of his individualistic concern to the broader concerns of all humanity.'[2] What makes a human being extraordinary? It is not merely social standing or fame. Those who fight for human rights and strive for the happiness of the downtrodden, even to the point of sacrificing themselves – these are the exceptional people.

This is why I respect the courageous citizens and many champions of humanity, including you and Dr King, who have fought long and hard for human rights and freedoms, risking their lives.

The struggle against the social evils of inequality, discrimination, poverty and violence is never-ending. Dr King sacrificed his life in this cause. His powerful example continues to inspire much courage and hope in those dedicated to justice and the cause of humanity.

I hope the youth – the next generation's leaders – will be inspired by the faith, wisdom and action of these immortal heroes and learn the lessons of this history. And I hope that these lessons will be engraved upon their young hearts. In this context, I believe our dialogue will be profoundly significant.

HARDING: Thank you, my brother. I have been looking forward to this because I feel that this discussion with you will be a wonderful opportunity to stimulate my own thinking and re-examine issues on a much deeper level.

Human existence includes the experiences of life and death. When I consider the life and death of individual human beings, I also am compelled to think of the life and death of societies. Today, more than forty years since the assassination of Martin Luther King Jr, I have a powerful premonition that we are at the beginning of a major transformation in American society.

IKEDA: Yes, and a symbol of this major transformation in American society is the appearance of President Barack Obama. In February 2008, when Mr Obama was considered the most likely presidential nominee of the Democratic Party, you stated in an interview with a Japanese newspaper, *The Mainichi Shimbun*:

> To his supporters, Mr Obama is the creator of a new America . . . I am sure that [Dr King] would have been very happy about Obama's surge in popularity. I think that he would have seen Obama's breakthrough as the magnificent next step on the journey toward the society about which he could only dream.[3]

Then, in January 2009, President Obama was sworn into office and thus took on the considerable hopes and aspirations of the American people. How do you view this tidal wave of change that is spreading across America?

HARDING: When I ponder the origins of what is currently happening in America – the Obama phenomenon – I am compelled to trace its beginnings to Martin Luther King and to the hundreds of thousands of magnificently ordinary women and men who were his co-workers. They led the post-World War II movement to expand democracy in America, known as the civil rights movement.

Mr Obama appeared on the scene long after the height of the civil rights movement, representing a new opportunity for young people to participate more in the ongoing struggle for the expansion of democracy, following in the steps of King and his comrades. This is the scenario in America today.

I'm happy that Mr Obama has focused on the goal of 'continu[ing] on the path of a more perfect Union'.[4] With these words, Obama has breathed the spirit embodied in the Preamble to the US Constitution[5] into the hearts of people who too often have completely forgotten it. He has thus rekindled their passion for justice and a transformed nation.

IKEDA: The Preamble extols the nation's founding ideals with the words 'We the People of the United States, in Order to form a more perfect Union . . .' In March 2008, President Obama, then a candidate, delivered a historic speech titled 'A More Perfect Union', in which he asserted that his mission was to 'continue the long march of those who came before us, a march for a more just, more equal, more free, more caring and more prosperous America'.[6] He called out to his fellow Americans to join him in creating a more perfect America – an America without the scourge of racial prejudice.

Describing himself as the 'son of a black man from Kenya and a white woman from Kansas . . . [who has] brothers, sisters, nieces, nephews, uncles and cousins, of every race and every hue, scattered across three continents',[7] Mr Obama advocated for racial harmony and reconciliation in his presidential acceptance speech. This moved many people.

HARDING: Today in America, many people have forgotten or are completely unaware that the primary purpose of our nation is not to build more efficient cars or refrigerators or more smart bombs. Rather, our fundamental task must be to 'form a more perfect Union'.

I am delighted that, by raising this issue, Barack Obama has opened up the opportunity for younger generations to discover something meaningful to which they can commit their lives. This is indeed the most important development to emerge in the United States since the civil rights movement in the 1950s and 1960s.

Mr Obama understands that he is an heir to the legacy of King and the movement. He has reminded people that the civil rights movement did not end with King's assassination, nor did it end with the legal recognition of the rights of black people. He has also reminded people that forming a 'more perfect Union' is an ongoing endeavour to which we all must commit ourselves for our entire lives and for the life of this nation.

Large numbers of Americans thus became wildly enthusiastic about Mr Obama's candidacy, his message inspiring the possibility of a new movement emerging in this country – a movement to recreate the country.

IKEDA: And the march to create a 'more perfect Union' called for by President Obama does not simply stop on the shores of the United States. The struggle for social justice – the struggle to win true freedom and equality – is a major challenge and goal for all humanity. As long as people are discriminated against, oppressed, and treated contemptuously anywhere in the world, we cannot rest; we must continue to seek a more perfect solidarity for all humankind. As Dr King astutely observed, 'Injustice anywhere is a threat to justice everywhere.'[8]

The essence of the Buddhist teachings lies in the unceasing struggle against threats to justice and in the quest to realize a peaceful world and the happiness and welfare of humanity. We must struggle decisively against the diabolical forces that cause human misery and threaten the dignity of life – this is the fundamental ideal on which the peace and human rights movement of the Soka Gakkai International is based. This is an eternal, never-ending struggle.

More Than Commander in Chief

HARDING: Wherever possible, we need to keep reminding President Obama that, even though he broke through the racial barrier to become president, racial discrimination is still alive. And we must, each of us, uproot traces of prejudice from our own hearts and actions.

We must also keep reminding our president that materialism is still one of the greatest poisons of American life. Dr King and his companions in the struggle worked tirelessly to liberate us from the darkness of the three evils of racism, materialism and militarism.

We must continually remind Mr Obama to turn toward his best self. When he is at his best, he can then embody the message of Dr King and the movement to expand democracy.

For someone such as Mr Obama, who has achieved the highest office in the nation, it may be difficult to continue progressing toward his highest self. However, I know that much of his best self was cultivated when he worked as a community organizer supporting grassroots democracy and standing with ordinary people to support them and help improve their situations.

I know that his mother insisted that his childhood education include the history of black-led movements to transform America. I am convinced that one of our major tasks as American citizens is to remind ourselves and our president of the sources of his best self.

IKEDA: The key concept of this new era will be 'grassroots democracy'. The citizenry and community are the starting points.

After graduating from Columbia University in 1983, President Obama moved to Chicago, where, as you said, he worked as a community organizer, sharing in the travails of the people and doing his utmost to improve their lives. The kind of leader people seek today continually strives to develop his or her highest self.

Essentially, the government, the nation and leaders all exist to serve the people. Many people have great expectations for this president, based on his experiences and history of standing up for ordinary people.

Have you ever given President Obama any advice?

HARDING: During the 2008 presidential campaign, I sent Mr Obama a message through a mutual friend:

> If you win the election and become president, don't spend much time trying to prove to the country how qualified you are to be commander in chief. Instead, remind us and yourself how qualified you are to be community organizer in chief. We need that much more.

My message was half playful but also serious. I repeated the essence of my message in an open letter to my president.[9]

IKEDA: The US Constitution confers on the president the power and authority to be commander in chief of the Army, Navy and National Guard, but I am sure that most people would rather President Obama's image not be that of the top military commander in charge of conducting wars.

HARDING: That's right. My feeling was that this is not the image a democratic nation needs to have of its leader – it's the image of a dictator. I had thus hoped he would focus on playing the role of community organizer in chief.

The role of the community activist is to help us understand that militarism leads to the destruction of communities at home and abroad. This was something that my brother Dr King understood well.

IKEDA: Local communities are the foundation on which people build their lives and the environment in which they create social solidarity and the bonds that nurture democracy. Nationalism that tends to worship '*our* people' and '*our* country' severs the ties among people and weakens their power.

The Soka Gakkai's first president and the originator of value-creating education, Tsunesaburo Makiguchi, a great educator and geographer, stood up against Japan's oppressive military authorities during World War II and, as a result, was thrown into prison, where he died.[10] Mr Makiguchi maintained that it is important for people to be aware of three levels of citizenship. First, that individuals are inhabitants of an immediate community, where they are deeply rooted. Second, that they also belong to a national community. Third, that they are global citizens, acting out the drama of their lives on the world stage.

An aware citizen pays special attention to the relationship between oneself and others, as well as that between oneself and the natural environment, and lives as a responsible participant in society. To be a global citizen means to have an enlightened, humanistic consciousness, a global perspective and to live as a responsible member of the global community.

Mr Makiguchi thus saw both the local community and the global community as the secure foothold that enables citizens to resist the evils of nationalism. He pointed out that in both the local and global community, we must get along as good neighbours and good citizens, deepen mutual understanding and work toward mutual harmony and benefit.

Josei Toda, the Soka Gakkai's second president, was imprisoned with President Makiguchi. He survived the ordeal and carried on the wishes of his predecessor, launching a struggle after the war for the cause of peace and humanity.

Dr King started his struggle for human rights at about the same time that, in Japan's Kansai area, I was also struggling for the sake of a people's movement, one aiming to transform society based on Buddhist principles and philosophy. As Josei Toda's disciple, I stood at the head of this people's movement for social change. Consequently, I was targeted with baseless criticism and slander, and, as a method of persecution, arrested on false charges of election law violations. After a long court battle to prove my innocence, I was finally vindicated by a ruling in my favour.

We of the Soka Gakkai International also feel a strong empathy with the resolute stance taken by you and Dr King against war.

HARDING: I hope to see President Obama keep thinking about how he can move himself more and more away from the path of militarism and toward a focus on building community, not only in this country but all over the world. This is the essence of Dr King's message.

As long as President Obama does not lose sight of his best self, he will be the one to manifest Dr King's message. However, he cannot succeed unless we help him in this effort. Indeed, it is our democratic responsibility to remind him and ourselves that the ways of war, the ways of drones, the ways of Special Forces are not the ways of building a 'more perfect Union' and not the ways of Martin Luther King.

IKEDA: Dr King likened the world to one large family, admonishing that we are a 'family unduly separated in ideas, culture, and interests who, because we can never again live without each other, must learn, somehow, in this one big world, to live with each other'.[11] As Dr King urged, we must learn from history and proceed down the road toward peace and coexistence. We must never again wage foolish war.

You were born in 1931, Dr King was born in 1929, and I was born in 1928. So, the three of us belong to a generation that lived through World War II. Former Soviet president Mikhail Gorbachev, who ended the Cold War, was also born in 1931. In my dialogue with him, he emphatically stated that our generation of 'wartime children' must expose the foolishness, inhumanity and absurdity of war.[12]

Our generation, having experienced the tragedies of war, is completely justified in our yearning for peace and also has an enormous responsibility to future generations. As we proceed in our dialogue, I want to discuss the theme of peace in detail.

You previously pointed out that, even now in American society, racial discrimination has yet to be extinguished. How would you compare America when you were growing up to America today?

Colourization of the Country

HARDING: In short, the main difference is that we have had a tremendous influx of immigrants to this country. This has meant a massive increase in people of colour and an increase in their proportion relative to the entire population. The colourization of this country is a major difference between the America of today and the post-World War II period.

IKEDA: Certainly, most immigrants coming to the United States in the pre-war period were from Europe. But after the war, there was a rapid increase in immigrants from Asia and Latin America. I have heard that by 2007, non-whites – blacks of African descent, Hispanics, Asians and so forth – already exceeded 100 million. This means that one-third of the US population was non-white. And given the rapid increase in Hispanic immigrants, the prediction was that this trend would continue.[13]

HARDING: Before the 1960s, based on the white supremacist ideal, US immigration law restricted the entry of people of colour. But partly as a result of the civil rights movement, a new immigration law was enacted in 1965.[14] This new law lifted racial restrictions on immigration.

The civil rights movement was advanced primarily by black

people, and it opened the way for other people of colour to come to this country. It is an important memory that ought to be reflected on as we make our way in this new multiracial America. It means that we African Americans and our allies have been crucial participants in opening our country to a new identity revealed by the most recent census reports[15] – a multiracial identity in which people of colour are becoming the new majority in America.

This requires much new thinking about who we, non-whites and whites, are and what our roles in this new nation will be. It requires much courage, creativity and imagination. It requires a process of rethinking that will likely be difficult for all of us, but we must engage one another in the work of reimagining and recreating America.

IKEDA: Walt Whitman, the people's poet, resoundingly celebrated this ideal America:

> *Come, I will make the continent indissoluble,*
> *I will make the most splendid race the sun ever yet*
> *shone upon,*
> *I will make divine, magnetic lands,*
> *With the love of comrades,*
> *With the life-long love of comrades.*[16]

Ever since my youth, Whitman has been one of my favourite poets, whose work I have loved reading time and time again.

Witnessing the turbulent events of his day – including the outbreak of the Civil War, the abolition of slavery and the assassination of President Abraham Lincoln – Whitman extolled this ideal of democracy and this new race of people linked by bonds of friendship and liberty that would emerge from it. Many of my American friends champion the ideals of this great poet as their own.

HARDING: Whitman has also been a long-time favourite of mine. One reason that he is so appealing is his superb ability to celebrate this country's democratic possibilities in verse. He believed profoundly in the potential for democracy in America. He also fervently insisted that the hard work of building democracy should be the most serious concern for the life of the country. Part of this work is the creation of a common history that will help us to understand our present and envision our future.

For instance, when I share the story of the civil rights movement, I have to tell about the long, and often cruel, bloodstained history that led up to it. Yet it is impossible to adequately convey the fears and apprehensions of black people in the last decades of the nineteenth century, many of whom worried – even after the abolition of slavery and the ratification of the Thirteenth Amendment to the US Constitution[17] – that the return of slavery remained a possibility.

That is to say, African Americans knew that for many white people in those days, it was impossible to imagine living in a country in which black people were not enslaved. Many whites felt that they at least needed clear signs and symbols of white power, white dominance and white supremacy to feel that all was right with the country.

IKEDA: Resulting from this feeling were the numerous discriminatory Jim Crow laws,[18] which existed in the Southern states before the Civil War and persisted all the way up until 1964. After the Civil War, the Civil Rights Act of 1875 prohibited discrimination in public facilities, including in hotel accommodations and on public transportation. In response, many Southern states quickly enacted a series of repulsive Jim Crow laws permitting discrimination in public accommodations. In 1896, the Supreme Court of the United States handed down a ruling endorsing racial segregation. After that, the bitter struggle continued against this discriminatory social system.

HARDING: That was how all kinds of terrorist groups – like the Ku Klux Klan – emerged to target black people, who were absolutely determined not to accept a return of slavery.

So was written the long history of the struggle between white society, which wanted to maintain its dominance and claim to superiority, and black society, which in response desired even more to be free. Blacks demonstrated a firm resolve to be regarded as Americans in their own right, always determined to create their own definition of 'American'.

Dr King was raised in the region of the country that most clearly revealed this antagonism and strife between blacks and whites but also most clearly the black commitment to create a 'more perfect Union'.

IKEDA: Atlanta saw some of the fiercest fighting in the Civil War and was known for some of the worst, most violent racial discrimination. Dr King was raised the child of a Baptist minister in Atlanta. After graduating from Atlanta's Morehouse College, one of the nation's most prestigious colleges for African Americans, he advanced to a theological seminary in Pennsylvania and, following in his father's footsteps, became a Baptist minister himself. Later, he earned his doctorate in theology from Boston University and devoted himself completely to the civil rights movement in the South.

I have heard that Dr King once told his good friend Harvey Cox that he actually wanted to be a theology and religion professor. However, he ultimately chose the arduous path of leading the civil rights movement.

HARDING: One of the reasons I have profound admiration for Dr King is that when he finished his doctorate at Boston University, he was well qualified to become a pastor of a large, comfortable congregation in any of the northern states, but instead, he and his wife, Coretta Scott King, returned to the South to put all their efforts into bringing about change on their native ground.

Black people living in the South struggled long after the abolition of slavery to be truly free. Because of this history, black people, at the grassroots community level, are grateful to Dr King.

It will be most important to link Mr Obama not only to the abolition of slavery and the civil rights movement but also to that long and bloody history leading to the present. We can see this in his family history. During the peak of the civil rights movement, when Barack's mother and father met and fell in love, there were many states in which they would not have been allowed to marry legally and where they literally could have been killed for their relationship. We must absolutely never forget that these conditions existed in our country well into the post-World War II years.

IKEDA: President Obama was born in 1961 in an era when the civil rights movement was surging, and the flames of war in Vietnam were spreading. It was in August 1963 in Washington, DC, that Dr King delivered his famous 'I Have a Dream' speech during the March on Washington for Jobs and Freedom. Soon after, four young girls were killed in the bombing of a Baptist church in Birmingham, Alabama. And three months after the march, President John F. Kennedy was assassinated.

In the midst of this stormy period of raging violence, Dr King fearlessly declared, 'I still have a dream, because, you know, you can't give up in life.'[19] The power of Dr King's unyielding convictions – the power of hope to win over every difficulty – is sorely needed in today's world.

You, too, have stated that our greatest challenge is to restore a sense of hope. I could not agree with you more. Hope is powerful. If we proceed forward with hope, a path will surely open before us. We will then resolutely open the way toward a new, more promising future.

HARDING: My sense is that many hopes and possibilities are emerging in America today. The road that America must take leads toward a new frontier.

And so we must ask ourselves: Do we have what it takes to create and walk down this new road, and are we prepared to make the most of the journey?

Dangerous crisis and great opportunity always coexist, and today we are confronting both. Now is our golden opportunity to seize the challenge before us. So, I say again and again to myself, to my students, to my fellow citizens and to my president: Let us give our greatest gifts and energies to the work of creating and occupying the path toward a 'more perfect Union'.

CONVERSATION TWO

A Brilliant Test of Human Nature

IKEDA: Thank you so much for visiting Soka University of America on a number of occasions. It has been of profound significance to our university's history to welcome you, a great advocate and activist for peace and human rights. As the university founder, I am grateful.

The students have been thrilled by your friendly, accessible manner. True democracy begins with dialogue, and the students have been sincerely moved by your humanistic philosophy, shared with fervent passion.

HARDING: Thank you. My visits to your university have been prompted by my desire for a clearer sense of your thoughts and feelings. A great way to accomplish this is by visiting Soka University of America, where you have invested so many of the best hopes and dreams of your life. Thanks to all the good people at SUA, I have felt encouraged and energized by my visits.

IKEDA: I'm happy to hear that and hope that you will feel free to visit often. Your visits will be inspiring and enlightening beyond measure for our students. I want to proceed with the thought that many young people, including our SUA students, will be participating, in a sense, in our current dialogue.

The struggle for human rights in the United States has a long, esteemed history. Today, as we face a major transition in this struggle, you have expressed your great hopes for the new leadership offered by President Obama to unify a diverse population and create a harmonious, peaceful society.

HARDING: It is most important for President Obama, as a self-identified black man, to bear witness to our country's history as it relates to the black experience. At the same time, the fact that he is the first black president of the United States is only one aspect of his presidency. My greatest hope for Obama is that he will be the first president to join with local communities to improve the lives of all Americans, especially in the poorest and most neglected parts of the nation.

IKEDA: Your expectations come across loud and clear. The point is to make local communities the basis for establishing ties among people of differing ethnic, economic and cultural backgrounds. After all, isn't this precisely the firm foundation that makes democracy strong?

The French political philosopher and historian Alexis de Tocqueville, who travelled the United States in the 1830s, commented in his well-known *Democracy in America* (1835):

> If America ever experiences great revolutions, they will be instigated by the presence of blacks on American soil: that is to say, it will not be the equality of social conditions but rather their inequality which will give rise to them.[1]

Tocqueville's American tour took place before slavery's

abolition. He insightfully predicted that 'great revolutions' would emerge from the social upheaval of oppressed people seeking dramatic change.

At any rate, with the election of the first African-American president, we have turned a page and entered a new era in American history.

HARDING: In order to realize a true democracy, every generation must be engaged in starting at the beginning and redoing the entire enterprise, making changes one after another, creating it anew.

Thomas Jefferson, the third president of the United States and author of the Declaration of Independence, cautioned that the democratic experiment is an imperfect one and can be made better only by those who participate in the experiment. This indicates that a major responsibility is placed on us.

Obama has embarked on this journey toward a better democracy, and one thing is clear to us: We, the American people, chose him as our leader.

We need to ask ourselves some questions: Can we steadfastly stand by Obama? Can we stand up with him? Can we spur him on, embrace him, challenge him and present him with everything that he needs to carry out his mission? Can we remember with him what is our truest mission? President Obama has been chosen by the people to be our leader and encourager in the historic American mission of creating a 'more perfect Union'. At our best, we understand that the realization of democracy depends on each of us.

IKEDA: The will of the people and citizen action are the keys to democracy. In order for society and the nation to proceed in the right direction, the people must be wise and united.

Dr King astutely observed, 'When an individual is no longer a true participant, when he no longer feels a sense of responsibility to his society, the content of democracy is emptied.'[2] The realization of true democracy depends upon a transformation in the consciousness of each person. Dr King articulates an important issue that must be addressed, not only by the United States but by all countries, if we are to build the new world of the future.

You were born and raised in New York City in the early 1930s, when the world was in the midst of the Great Depression. Immersed in your community, you grew strong and resolute as you experienced the joys and sorrows of the people whose lives were impacted by that economic crisis.

What especially indelible memories from your childhood do you have of your mother and father?

HARDING: My parents were together only until I was about four, and then they divorced. After that, I was an only child raised by a single mother. We lived in what would now be called poverty and therefore qualified to receive public welfare.

In addition to her jobs as a domestic servant and hotel maid, my mother supported us by taking in laundry from various families. Ever since I could remember, my mother worked hard every day. She devoted all her energy, love and wisdom to raising and supporting me.

My mother made it clear to me that she had the highest expectations for me. Growing up in a poor village in Barbados (West Indies), she had only completed eighth grade and had not been to high school before migrating to the United States in the 1920s. This is why she did everything she could, taking any kind of job to make sure that I had educational opportunities. It is also important to note that my mother and I received much emotional and spiritual support from the members of the small Protestant congregation that was a crucial part of my life in Harlem – the Victory Tabernacle Seventh Day Christian Church.

IKEDA: She was a magnificent, praiseworthy mother. I have the highest regard for the pride that fills your voice when you speak of the hardships she endured for your sake. She must have been very proud of you. I am sure that your successes made her happy, and that she felt your victories were her own.

HARDING: Thank you. Even now, I distinctly remember the boarding house in Harlem where we lived during my childhood. The house was owned by the minister of another small church. My mother attended the church meetings that were held there on the main floor every week.

During that period, we had an experience that became one of my mother's favourite memories. One year at Thanksgiving, when most American families enjoy a special Thanksgiving dinner, we could not hope to have anything like that. However, a kind social worker brought us some food for a complete meal. My mother was elated, and she impressed on my young heart that 'God takes care of his own, and so he would never forsake us.'

IKEDA: What a touching story. I can see that your mother's love-filled words left a deep impression on your heart and have become a cherished memory. In every era and in every country, motherhood is the essential foundation of our existence.

I also cherish things that my mother said to me. Once, just before I started school, when I was struggling with ill health, my mother pointed to the pomegranate tree in our yard and said:

> Look at that pomegranate tree. It's supposed to dislike salt, wind, and sandy soil, like what we have around here, but still it blooms and bears fruit every year. You may be weak now, but you're sure to grow strong some day.

As I lay in bed, feverish with pneumonia, her words gave me hope.

Then, when my father became unable to work because of his rheumatism, and one economic hardship after another befell our family, my mother would cheerfully joke with us, buoying our spirits by saying, 'We may be poor, but we're grand champions at being poor.' I will never forget how much my mother's smiling face rescued all of us from our troubles.

HARDING: She must have been a wonderful person.

I have many memories of the hardships and relative poverty we experienced, but I almost never felt a sense of desperation or sadness. That's because my mother and I always had the warmth and support of the members of our church community, and they gave us a helping hand. I will always remember the people we met in our little church. They embraced, encouraged and nurtured me during my childhood. The place that had the most influence in creating the spiritual foundation of my life was the church community.

I am always aware that, as human beings, we need to have roots. It was my mother's love and support as well as the kindness and nurturing of the people in the church and community, my extended family, that deeply grounded me in that place.

IKEDA: It seems that you were raised in a community that was a loving network of people. More and more people these days are seeking to build communities characterized by strong, functional relationships, because in that kind of community, people come together to care for and raise children.

For example, when children are playing in the park, if the parents aren't nearby, the neighbours can look out for the children and give them advice. Or, at times, they may scold a child as if he or she were their own. This is how it used to be in Japan, and people thought this was natural. It was expected community behaviour.

However, today this kind of scenario is rare, and a weakening of local capacity for guidance and the disintegration of a sense of community are increasingly serious problems. The sense of community, especially in urban areas, is weakening. In this context, Soka Gakkai International activities, based on Buddhist humanism rooted in 'transcending all differences',[3] focus on expanding ties of friendship and trust on the community level. And, as you say, close relationships among members of a community are increasingly important for people to feel grounded and have a sense of rootedness.

Growing up in that kind of community, what was your school experience like?

A First Step

HARDING: I remember that I always loved school. It was a place where I was appreciated, praised and encouraged. It was a joy for me to go to school.

However, a few times my conduct was not the most desirable. In fact, on one of my report cards, the teacher wrote, 'Talks too much in class to others', and gave me a C for conduct!

IKEDA: Evidently, you were lively and full of energy. What were your favourite classes?

HARDING: I had a profound interest in learning about people. I particularly loved history. I owe this to wonderful teachers who stimulated my interest in the field.

When I was in the sixth grade, I became interested in model airplanes and loved building them. At one point, my science teacher entered my model airplane into a citywide competition, and I won a prize. My teacher was so excited when he came back and told me about the prize I had won. From that point onward, I became completely enthralled with aeronautical engineering – even though I didn't know what that was.

IKEDA: You were blessed with an excellent teacher who inspired you to learn, a first step toward becoming an eminent historian. Your anecdote about your model airplane prize is heart-warming, reminding me once again how, when it comes to education, praising children helps them grow and develop. Were there any other teachers who left a lasting impression on you?

HARDING: My life has been so enriched by many wonderful teachers. Mrs Irene Berger was my high school advisor. I never took a class from her, but she became a dear friend. We kept in touch long after I graduated. She was one of the people who saw something in me and believed that I had potential.

Mrs Berger not only encouraged me, she also invited my mother to visit the school, and she even invited us to her home. Thanks to her, I got a part-time job, which helped our household considerably.

President Ikeda, what memories do you have of your teachers?

IKEDA: Let me see. I still remember the praise I received from my homeroom teacher for a composition I wrote the year I entered primary school. It was then that my hope of perhaps someday becoming a writer or newspaper reporter began to grow.

When I was in the fifth or sixth grade, my homeroom teacher, Kohei Hiyama, once spread out a world map and asked each of us to point to a place that we wanted to visit. I pointed to the middle of Asia, and he exclaimed: 'Look! You pointed to Dunhuang. Did you know that there are many magnificent treasures there?' That is when I first became fascinated with China's desert museum of ancient Buddhist relics in Dunhuang. At that time, I never dreamt that one day I would talk about the Silk Road with the world-renowned scholar of Dunhuang research, Chang Shuhong, and publish a book with him.[4]

Once, when our class went on a field trip, I bought food and drinks for all my friends with the meagre spending money my mother had scraped together for me. Observing this, Mr Hiyama quietly took me aside and said: 'Ikeda, you should be buying presents for your father and mother, not only treating all your friends. Your older brothers are all away at war, aren't they?' He quietly slipped me a little spending money. Even now, I feel the same warm appreciation I felt that day.

I can tell from your stories that you, too, were surrounded by many warm, wonderful people. Indeed, a person who lives amid such warm relationships is blessed with a rich, satisfying life.

Can you share any unforgettable experiences from your childhood that led to your later involvement in the civil rights movement?

HARDING: I have given this issue a great deal of thought. I don't have a clear recollection of exactly when I first encountered serious racial discrimination. I do, however, recall several experiences. Among them were the times when many of the people in my extended family of the church gave me this counsel: 'Remember, Vincent, as a black boy, you're going to have to be twice as good as whites in order to be considered equal.' There was a seed planted, and their advice guided my life.

Another experience was when I was in junior high school. At the time, our Harlem church was a short distance from a small park. Between the morning service and lunch as well as between afternoon services, we children would always walk to the park to run around and play. One day, three of us set out for the park and were playing there for a while when we saw four or five young white men, probably in high school.

One of us innocently asked them, 'What are you doing here?'

One of them answered, 'We're hunting.'

When asked, 'What are you hunting?' he responded, 'We're hunting niggers!'

In a flash, the three of us jumped up and ran away as fast as we could.

That was the extent of my earliest brush with racial discrimination. I have not had the kind of dramatic and unpleasant experiences with white racism that so many others encountered.

IKEDA: That's a disturbing story. But it's moving that the guiding principle you adopted for your life was to be 'twice as good'.

Your experience in the park reminds me of the first time I travelled to the United States and visited Chicago. It was in October 1960, and I was strolling through Lincoln Park, chatting with friends, when we witnessed a group of white children refusing to let a black child play ball with them. Making the situation even worse, an older white man sitting on a nearby bench yelled at the boy, sending him running away downcast and disheartened.

It all happened in an instant, but I felt that I had glimpsed the dark underside of American society at that time. When I saw the resentment and indignation in the eyes of that black youth, I swore to myself that I would devote my life to creating a society that the boy could love, of which he could be proud.

We must not permit discrimination of any sort. Our Soka Gakkai International movement is based on the fundamental principles of Buddhism – peace, equality and compassion – that compel us to build a society protecting human rights and the dignity of all life.

Getting back to our topic, you met your mother's expectations and dedicated yourself to your studies, graduating as class valedictorian and going on to the City College of New York. By the way, Townsend Harris, founder of that prestigious college, is well known in Japan as the first US consul-general and minister to Japan.

You studied history at City College. You mentioned that you have always been interested in history, but can you say more about what led you to choose history as your speciality?

Sharing Our Stories

Harding: It's probably because, when I was a child, I was fascinated by fairy tales, and I have always had a love of story. When I was applying to the Columbia University Graduate School of Journalism, in response to a question about why I wanted to go into journalism, I wrote, 'I want to tell the story of my people.'

Another reason is that I had the good fortune of having some excellent history teachers in college. They aroused my interest in the great variety of stories about how human beings have wrestled with the human condition.

Ikeda: Certainly, the field of history is not simply the recording of historical fact. It reveals the stories of individuals as well as the stories of societies. The English word *history* includes the word *story*, and when we trace the origins of these words, we find that they were used at one time interchangeably. In China, by the way – a civilization that has always placed a high value on recorded history – there is both the tradition of official histories of national events, of the dynasties, and an equally strong, parallel tradition of biographies, focusing on individuals' lives.

Learning from history is, ultimately, a process of searching for a fundamental way to sustain society and understand human nature more profoundly. President Toda often emphasized having a historical perspective, repeatedly telling young people, 'You must make a serious effort to learn from history!' and 'Deepen your historical perspective!'

Harding: This is my thought, too. Our creative capacity emerges from telling stories. And I suggest that we are already living inside our own stories, as if we were storied into being. In the same way that food and water are essential to our survival, stories are also essential. Gathering together to tell stories is absolutely necessary for every human society.

The psychiatrist Carl Jung maintained that when a person tells us about his or her dream, that dream no longer belongs only to the teller. It belongs also to us, the listeners. If that is the case, might this not apply to stories as well?

I maintain that for every country in the world to develop a healthy democracy, we must share our stories as well as listen carefully to the stories of others.

IKEDA: As human beings, we share our past, exist together in the present, and aspire to create a common future. And we come to know that, as we have our own precious stories, other people likewise have their own valuable stories. The foundation of mutual understanding that emerges through dialogue is the lifeblood that animates democracy. To develop a close, understanding community, we need opportunities for intimate, mutually inspiring dialogue that enables each person to share the story of his or her life.

In the 192 countries and territories in which our movement has been established, the Soka Gakkai International's custom is to hold small group discussion meetings. At each of these meetings, the members of that community gather to learn about Buddhism and talk about their experiences. This provides an opportunity for people to tell the story of their lives – the story in which they play the leading role. The other participants applaud in support and offer encouragement.

In the United States, when the members discuss their faith experiences, they say they are 'sharing' their stories, not just 'telling' them. They share one another's joys and sorrows. At times, the members are moved to tears when they hear about another's sadness, and they also become jubilant when they share in another's joys. It is an energizing experience, enabling people to develop the courage to confront their worries and carry on with creating their lives.

Each person is indeed living his or her story. This is a story that one has chosen and in which one plays the leading role. Woven together, these individual stories create the grand story that is human history.

In a democracy, the people play the leading role. Therefore, democracy flowers from the fertile ground of people who live their own lives believing that 'My heart is the protagonist in a victorious life.'

HARDING: Hearing many different stories helps us to understand our origins, where we've come from. But on a more poetic level, these stories help us to understand how we are connected to one another. It is this thought that makes us understand that we are all parts of one whole – there is no real separation.

This means that separation and division are nothing more than illusions. Our various stories indeed call attention to the connectivity that exists among human beings.

IKEDA: Isn't America, the land of the free, the stage on which individuals can create, perform and forge a victory in their own ideal stories?

If you had the chance to choose the country in which your life story would be told, would you still choose America?

HARDING: I feel blessed to have been born in this country, in the time and in the place that I was born. I feel that this country is endowed with some kind of divine potential. We enjoy the blessing of being a community of immigrants, a gathering place for people belonging to every race on Earth. Each and every person who has come to America should not think of him- or herself as having come to the endpoint of the journey; America is a place where everyone can make a new beginning.

I see this wonderfully rich and diverse gathering of human beings as a great strength as well as a brilliant test of human nature.

At the same moment, I cannot forget the profound tragedies built into the founding of our nation – the uprooting and destruction of so many of the indigenous peoples and the exploitation of the enslaved, imported population.

IKEDA: Yes, these are events that we must never allow ourselves to forget or to repeat.

Regarding the origins of the human race, recent genetic research tells us that the ancestors of humanity, having emerged in Africa, began their journey throughout the world about 50,000 years ago. In the course of this long journey, many different kinds of peoples evolved and populated every corner of the Earth. In each region, they put down roots and adapted to their respective environments, giving birth to a variety of philosophies, cultures and religions over countless generations. Now, it's as if all of these distinct peoples are reuniting in America and weaving a story of new encounters and connections. As you say, America is not an endpoint but rather a new beginning. Indeed, it is humanity's grand experiment.

HARDING: Let me say this with a slight bit of humour as well as something deeper: It's a way of testing the wisdom of God for making such a strange variety of beings, giving them all the capacities that we have, and then telling them to get together and figure out how to live together, how to love one another, how to share and how to bless one another and bless this world. I think of this as a reflection on America's potential.

IKEDA: The rich diversity of its people is one of the appeals of America and a source of all humanity's rich potential and creativity. I sincerely love America and am fascinated with this American dynamism. It was in America that I took the first step in my journey to seek world peace[5] and also intend to bring my life's work to its culmination, having founded Soka University of America as the main arena for my endeavours in the field of education. The underlying foundation supporting the diversity that flourishes in America is recognition of a shared humanity and affirmation of life.

Langston Hughes, known as the poet laureate of Harlem, had this to say about our humanity and the depths from which it springs: 'I've known rivers: / I've known rivers ancient as the world and older than the flow of human blood in human veins. / My soul has grown deep like the rivers.'[6]

Our focus should be life, the depths from which these rivers flow forth. The life of every person is profound and deserving of dignity and respect.

HARDING: Hughes is one of my favourite poets. Like Whitman, he focused on and celebrated the potential beauty of a multiracial, multi-ethnic American democracy.

IKEDA: When we can grasp the true nature of our lives, we realize we are all equal on this planet called Earth, spinning through the vast expanse of the universe. By awakening to this reality, we become more aware of the dignity of life, which is a humbling experience. This in turn makes it possible for us to redefine our own existence while genuinely respecting the lives of others. Then, together, we can proudly embrace our new identity as global citizens.

CONVERSATION THREE

The Coming of the New America

IKEDA: In June 1996, I was invited to the graduation ceremony of the University of Denver, an outstanding centre of learning in Colorado. I recall the panoramic and stunningly beautiful landscape, set near the eastern foothills of the majestic Rocky Mountains.

Thomas Hornsby Ferril (1896–1988), a Colorado poet laureate, wrote, 'Here is a land where life is written in water . . .'[1] I visited a city park in which the lake, named after Ferril, was as smooth and calm as a celestial mirror. There is no doubt that the city of Denver, which has been the forum for your activities for many years, holds a special fascination for all its visitors.

Parallelling the beauty of the natural setting, the most striking memories imprinted upon my heart are my discussions with distinguished friends such as University of Denver Professor Ved Nanda and you.

HARDING: Something about the magnificence of this place exerts a powerful force that resonates within me. I remember a book, *Song of the Sky*, by Guy Murchie. The vastness of our sky constantly strikes me as powerful. This sense of the boundless expanse of the universe creates a perpetual resonance in my heart. Thirty years have already passed since I first came to this place, and Denver's natural environment has had some effect on the development of my character.

Each day, the mountains never cease to astonish me. To walk in Denver and, simply by turning a few blocks one way or the other, to suddenly have the magnificent Rocky Mountains open up before you is a powerfully transformative experience. I am moved when I gaze upon these mountains.

Then I flash upon this thought: I wonder what the human beings who first came to this place thought when they witnessed this mountain range. I imagine that it was no ordinary encounter.

IKEDA: Tsunesaburo Makiguchi observed in his major work, *A Geography of Human Life*, that mountains serve to moderate human nature and elevate the human heart. He also refers to the Rocky Mountains in this work.

When I attended the University of Denver graduation, I was honoured to receive an honorary doctorate of education. The moon auspiciously rose upon the ceremony, held outdoors under the clear, blue Denver sky. On that occasion, I was unexpectedly asked to make a few impromptu remarks, and so I came up with a brief comment:

> The sun is shining brilliantly. The moon, too, is shining upon all of you. The sun symbolizes passion; the moon, intellect. And the Rocky Mountains, with their air of unshakable conviction, are watching over you.[2]

This was meant as my congratulations and best wishes for the graduates who were embarking, in high spirits, on their life journeys. I still remember fondly the warm applause I received from those promising young people on that occasion.

HARDING: Your story reminds me of when I went to Lincoln University, the African-American school in Pennsylvania, where Kwame Nkrumah, who eventually became leader of Ghana and the post-World War II anti-colonial movement in Africa, received his college degree many years ago. I was to receive an honorary degree, and my family had come with me. Unexpectedly, the university president asked me to give a talk of about ten minutes. My son leaned over and whispered humorously in my ear: 'She really doesn't know you, Daddy, does she? It takes you ten minutes just to get warmed up.' So, I completely understand how you must have felt. You rose to the occasion and produced a splendid poem.

IKEDA: The outdoor graduation was in itself a memorable, poetic occasion, like a great painting, embracing nature as a friend. I have always felt that the magnificence of nature stirs in the human heart a profound reverence for life. We are enveloped by the boundlessness of nature and the universe that nurtures us. This teaches us how foolish it is to quarrel and bicker with one another over trivialities. We learn the importance of re-examining ourselves with humility and respecting others' lives.

President Makiguchi observed in the work I mentioned, 'We can say that the mountains educate us and contribute to the kinds of persons we become.'[3] Majestic mountains have an enigmatic power to cultivate in us a magnanimous, broad-minded character.

Do you now consider Denver your home after living there for so many years?

HARDING: I moved to Denver when I was fifty. While I carry within myself a sense of the places where I previously lived, occasionally I have a strangely interesting sense of myself as a Denverite.

My identity is, even now, deeply rooted in New York. As I have already mentioned, Harlem is where my life began. Later, during the time I participated in the civil rights movement, our family lived in the South, so that place is still important to me. Chicago is also significant because it is where I met the woman who became my wife, Rosemarie Freeney, and it was where I encountered a religious community called the Mennonites – two important encounters in my life.

So I am not a Denverite in the same sense as many other people who have lived there for fifty years or more, but at the same time, I have great appreciation for Denver and the state of Colorado.

IKEDA: I have certainly felt the warm, hometown hospitality with which Denver welcomes visitors and newcomers.

More than 130 years ago, Walt Whitman set out on a journey from New Jersey through Missouri, Kansas and Colorado. Recalling his visit to Denver, he expressed his admiration, describing it as 'no doubt one of the greatest [cities] on the continent'.[4]

He also observed of Denver: 'It had something in its air that fascinated me – held me. I could never entirely shake off the desire to stop there – stay there – become part of that new country.'[5] I am sure that many travellers have shared the same feelings of amazement and wonder that Whitman felt.

HARDING: Whitman's comments bring up many thoughts.

First, I would like to go back and recall the experiences I had in the 1970s. I remember that, when I first came to Colorado, a friend took us out for a drive in the Rockies, from Denver over to the Western Slope. As we were driving through the mountains, I had the strangest experience: I suddenly felt a deep impression that I had lived in this place a long, long time ago, and that the history of these mountains was somehow related to me and my own history. I have no way of knowing what that meant, but it was such a powerful sense of reality, a sense of belonging, connected to the mountains and to the earliest human inhabitants.

IKEDA: It's the feeling of returning to one's spiritual home, isn't it? Of this magnificent landscape, Whitman wrote, 'These reckless heaven-ambitious peaks / These gorges, turbulent-clear streams, this naked freshness . . .'[6]

One could say that in Denver one feels the impact of nature, while its residents also radiate a sparkling humanity. The traditional culture of coexistence with nature nurtured there over many years is wonderful. Denver has achieved a remarkable degree of development and now is known as one of the most diverse, appealing cities in the United States.

HARDING: The aspect of Denver that intrigued me the most was something that my friend Maria Guajardo[7] emphasized. She told me about Denver's population, informing me that Latinos made up the major portion of the population, and that the percentage of whites was on the decline, while the black and long-time Asian populations, including the Japanese, remained relatively stable. Denver was a place where peoples with extremely incongruous and seemingly irreconcilable characteristics came together and learned to appreciate one another's differences and discover the commonalities they shared. That Denver was a kind of experimental laboratory appealed to me and Rosemarie. It is a preparation for the coming of the new America.

A Sense of Shared Identity

IKEDA: 'The coming of the New America' – what an amazing expression. Denver is indeed ahead of its time. I can see why your wife also loved Denver. Your city, the dazzling 'Queen City of the Plains', is popular as a tourist destination and is well-known as the venue for the G8 Summit held in 1997.

It was this summit that Russia attended for the first time as a fully participating member. As one who had called for participation of a diverse assembly of countries, not simply the G7, I felt this was a significant step forward.

Also to Denver's credit, the Denver International Airport, completed in 1995, is now one of the largest airports in the United States and a major hub for the movement of people and goods throughout North America. The 2008 Democratic National Convention, at which Obama was officially nominated as the Democratic Party candidate for president, was also held in Denver.

Your comment that Denver is a place where 'peoples with extremely incongruous and seemingly irreconcilable characteristics came together and learned to appreciate one another's differences' is important. In *A Geography of Human Life*, Mr Makiguchi made a major distinction between mountain ranges that run from north to south and those that lie along an east–west axis. He observed that the division between north and south, accentuated by climatic effects, is a major contributing factor to social and cultural differences between people living on the north versus the south side of a latitudinal mountain range. In contrast, longitudinal mountain ranges, which run from north to south, often do not impose a barrier to social integration of people living on the eastern and western sides of the mountain range. The Rocky Mountains, true to the rule, comprise a longitudinal mountain range on the American continent that can unify east and west.

HARDING: There are at least two other lessons that Denver teaches us. One lesson is that we human beings are diverse and are distinguished by major differences. The second lesson is that this diversity is a treasure. Our differences help us recognize and nurture the many commonalities we also share, all of which are essential to creating a sense of shared identity.

Most people agree that a positive and enlightened view does not obsess about differences. However, how one views these differences is important. Will they be used in a socially constructive way or in a divisive way? The people of Denver have given this matter a great deal of thought and, at their best, have created a wonderful social environment.

I recall a youth-based, community-building venture that our Veterans of Hope Project worked on in the summer of 2007,[8] when we brought together many black, white, Latino, Asian and Native American young people. For the majority of the youth, this two-week event was their first experience in cross-cultural communal living and learning. It was a tremendous challenge for the young people and sometimes a trying situation for the counsellors who stayed with them day and night. Nevertheless, the young people were all thrilled with their experience.

This kind of thing is what appeals to me about Denver – the possibilities for seeking ways to build a new human society, a society that acknowledges and honours our differences as Americans and as human beings, a country that sees our differences as beautiful building blocks for the New America.

IKEDA: Denver is characterized by a vital spirit and traditional culture of tolerance. The treatment of Japanese Americans there during World War II is one significant instance of the city's ethos. Since the West was first opened, Denver has had a close relationship to Japan. From the end of the nineteenth century through the beginning of the twentieth, many Japanese migrant labourers crossed the ocean to work in the coalmines and on the railroad, and they founded Denver's Japan Town.

Unfortunately, in December 1941 after the attack on Pearl Harbor, the Pacific War broke out. The Japanese military government pushed forward its attacks on areas in Asia and the Pacific region, driving many people into war.

President Franklin D. Roosevelt then made the decision to incarcerate Japanese Americans who had been living on the West

Coast. He had them forcibly interned in camps in various states in the interior of the country. Among all of the governors of the ten western states at that time, only Ralph L. Carr, Colorado governor, did not hesitate to express his acceptance of Japanese Americans and his resistance to racial discrimination and hatred.

Governor Carr insisted that Japanese Americans be treated with respect and humanity. When Japanese Americans arrived in Colorado at the Granada War Relocation Centre, commonly known as Camp Amache, there were many incidents of mob violence against them. Governor Carr appealed for restraint and contained the mobs:

> If you harm them, you must first harm me. I was brought up in small towns where I know the shame and dishonor of race hatred. I grew to despise it because it threatened the happiness of you and you and you.[9]

Governor Carr's determination and actions were criticized by many, but he resolutely stood up for his beliefs, speaking out with courage and commitment.

HARDING: By calling up and confronting the shameful and hate-filled memories of the past, Governor Carr acknowledged those memories of racial discrimination and declared that he had not obliterated them from his own memory. I find that many white people are unable to call up those memories or are afraid to call them up because of all that they imply, and so they come to believe that those memories do not exist. This is a dangerous amnesia.

IKEDA: Governor Carr advocated that Japanese Americans must be guaranteed their constitutional and human rights, like any other American citizens, but ultimately, the American public did not agree. In 1942, Governor Carr ran as a candidate for the US

Senate and was subjected to unrelenting criticism for his beliefs by opponents, full of animosity toward Japanese Americans. He lost by a narrow margin and never returned to politics.

More than half a century later, in 1999, Governor Carr was honoured by *The Denver Post* as an esteemed figure representing Colorado in the twentieth century. Governor Carr is someone to whom Japanese and Japanese Americans are indebted and whom they must not – or I should say, must *never* – forget.

A bust of Governor Carr has been installed in Sakura Square in downtown Denver, and I am sure that he watches over the people of the city. This demonstrates that history undeniably bears witness to the just, courageous actions of people of conscience. At the same time, this is a reminder of our duty to build a society that does so.

Dr King stated, 'Our hope for creative living in this world house that we have inherited lies in our ability to reestablish the moral ends of our lives in personal character and social justice.'[10] He also warned that unless human beings achieve a spiritual, moral awakening, we will end up destroying ourselves.

If we are to avoid proceeding foolishly toward self-destruction, we must learn, with humility, from our past mistakes and unwaveringly pursue the path of humanity and justice. In every age and in every country, this is the task and the challenge that we human beings must undertake.

Life Depends on Community

Harding: Some years ago, in our Veterans of Hope Project, which includes several oral histories, we interviewed a number of older Japanese-American citizens burdened by past memories. Among the interviewees were people who, for a long time, did not want to unearth memories of the hardships they suffered at the wartime internment camps. However, these people came to realize that by publicly recalling their experiences, they were sharing a precious treasure that advances democracy – and their recognition of this fact led them to make a valuable contribution to posterity.

I celebrate Governor Carr. At the same time, I again encourage all white people to shake off their fears and confront their history straight on. For it is by doing so that they – and all of us – can bravely proceed toward our common future.

Martin Luther King Jr Day, the annual celebration of Dr King's life – and the pro-democracy movement that he represented – affords us this opportunity. It was first celebrated as a holiday in 1986. I was then teaching at the Iliff School of Theology, located on the University of Denver campus, and Iliff had not yet planned any celebration.

At the time, I was team-teaching a class with two other professors, and they asked me to lead the class that fell on Martin Luther King Jr Day. I questioned the students in the class, all of whom were young children on 4 April 1968, when Martin was assassinated, and even younger during the early years of the southern-based black movement for the expansion of democracy in America. I especially wanted to hear from them about their memories of discussions in their families about what was happening then in the United States under the leadership of black people.

I will never forget the surprising and painfully honest comments of a white student in his forties. He remembered that the contents of family dinner-table discussions at that time were strictly determined by his father, and there was an unwritten rule that any topic related to race or social change would not enter the conversation. No one in the family was allowed to raise these issues. Nevertheless, since then, the student added, every time he heard a song from the black experience, he would cry inside. If we are ever to realize the kind of country we hope for, we must learn and speak and rejoice and cry about one another's history.

IKEDA: I have heard that now, every January, Martin Luther King Jr Day is celebrated in grand style in Denver as well as other places with events including parades. Dr King's journey took him to Denver, didn't it?

HARDING: Martin came to Denver twice, I think. (It was long before I moved to Denver.) Around ten years ago, a local Denver filmmaker made a fine documentary about King's visits. I was even more impressed by a wonderful sculpture of King created by a local artist and installed at a city park. The reason it was so powerful was that, while the film focused on Dr King in the context of his visits to Denver, the sculpture portrayed Dr King on the world stage: It did not limit his sphere to Denver or the United States but went beyond to show him and his companions in their struggle for human rights everywhere.

IKEDA: I understand that the statue of Dr King was installed in the city park at Ferril Lake in 2002. Surrounding Dr King are statues of his fellow warriors and champions of the human rights movement, such as Mahatma Gandhi; Frederick Douglass, the former slave who advocated for the abolition of slavery and the establishment of racial justice; Sojourner Truth, the black woman activist, also a former slave; and the well-known Rosa Parks (see Conversation Seven), often referred to as the mother of the civil rights movement.

These champions have brought much inspiration and illumination to the members of the Soka Gakkai International. For example, in January 1993, we hosted Rosa Parks at the Calabasas campus of Soka University of America[11] on the outskirts of Los Angeles. On that occasion, she joined our young men and women in singing 'We Shall Overcome'. This is one of the most treasured memories of our history. In May of the following year, she was kind enough to visit us at Soka University and Soka Women's College in Tokyo. I fondly recall talking about the history and spirit of the civil rights movement with Ms Parks on that occasion.

I have spoken to our youth about Sojourner Truth, who fought for the abolition of slavery, and commended her beliefs and bravery. And regarding Mahatma Gandhi, I was invited to speak at the Gandhi Smriti and Darshan Samiti, where I delivered a talk titled 'Toward a World without War – Gandhism and the Modern World'. Subsequently, the Rajiv Gandhi Institute for Contemporary Studies invited me to deliver a talk titled 'A New Humanism for the Coming Century'. Gandhi's concept of non-violence has been and continues to be an important stimulus in our own peace movement.

In this sense, it is my honour and pleasure to convey to the young people of the world the inspiring message that you and your great friend, the unrivalled Dr King, demonstrated through your lives and struggle for justice.

Incidentally, when I visited Denver, I was impressed by the warm hospitality shown us by the SGI-USA's Native American sisters and brothers. There is much we should learn from the rich culture and wisdom of Native Americans.

HARDING: After settling in Denver, Rosemarie and I spent much time with our Native American friends. Also, we took every opportunity to travel to nearby places, especially to Native American pueblos in New Mexico and to the northern part of the Dakota reservation, one of the places where the Sun Dance ceremony of the Great Sioux Nation is held.

When I think about the wisdom of these indigenous peoples, I think first that indigenous peoples everywhere remind us, with excellent examples, that life depends upon the building of community, and therefore it is absolutely essential to nurture the development of community wherever we live.

IKEDA: I understand that, beginning several thousand years ago, a variety of peoples lived in the area that is now Colorado. The indigenous wisdom of Native Americans offers many valuable lessons about community life, including the importance of intergenerational relationships – for example, the proverb 'It takes a whole village to raise a child.'

HARDING: The formation of communities is significant. Today, what we are trying to learn is whether all the 'development' that we have pursued during the Industrial Age – development that has often inflicted such damage on community – will lead to the realization of some kind of new, deeper and stronger sense of community.

I recently read a persuasive column contending that we have underestimated the role of friends in helping people to become healthy, to maintain their health, to recover from illness and also to learn how to grow old. Research conducted over the past decade shows that for most people, social networks of friends are most important to their physical and mental health.[12]

IKEDA: That's an important finding. According to research conducted at Harvard University's School of Medicine, one's general sense of happiness is influenced by the sense of happiness of others in one's social sphere. For example, if you have a happy friend who lives within a mile of where you live, the possibility of your experiencing a sense of happiness is 25 per cent, while if your happy friend lives in the neighbourhood, your chances of feeling happy increase to 34 per cent.[13]

This sense of happiness is conveyed from friend to friend, expanding like ripples on the surface of a pond, spreading physical and mental health. This research holds important implications in considering the significance of local communities.

Creating open, enlightened community networks linking

people heart to heart is one of the most important tasks of our era. Buddhism repeatedly stresses the importance of friendship. Shakyamuni called everyone 'friend' without exception and even told one of his disciples, 'Verily the whole of this life in religion consists in righteous friendship, righteous intimacy, righteous association.'[14]

One aspect of *compassion* as taught in Buddhism is, in contemporary terms, *friendship*. Strengthening the spirit of harmonious coexistence – of the vibrant friendship that enables us to converse as equals and work together hand in hand, transcending self-interest, social status, race and religion – is the essential spirit of the Buddhist teachings.

HARDING: Jesus also spoke with people as equals and friends, rather than looking down on them from on high. Personally, when people call me *friend*, I strive to engage them in dialogue with an attitude of respect and equality.

IKEDA: Members of the Soka Gakkai International in Denver are engaged in promoting friendly dialogue with their fellow community members. For many years, they have, as a symbol of their appreciation and goodwill toward the community, planted cherry trees in Denver's parks and along its creeks. Today, the wider community also participates in planting the trees. When May comes, Denver citizens enjoy the cherry blossoms in full bloom, and it seems that the occasion symbolizes a sense of solidarity and goodwill among people of the community.

Denver's average winter temperature tends to be cold, and it was thought that it would be difficult to grow cherry trees there. Our friends in the SGI-USA carefully wrapped each and every tree with thermal tape during the winter season. As a result, the cherry trees thrived and blossomed magnificently each year.

Similarly, we would like to carefully nurture the next generation of promising young people who will bear responsibility for our future. We want to expand a forest of friendship. We believe that the firm foundation for creating an age of peace and humanity is established through encouraging each individual and engaging in sincere dialogue.

HARDING: The cherry trees are beautiful gifts to our city. Your thoughts about the next generation of young people are also encouraging. I wonder what the best human equivalent of 'thermal tape' might be.

CONVERSATION FOUR

Extraordinary Character

IKEDA: Friendship is life's treasure. It is the ultimate flowering of human experience and the power behind a peaceful society. You and your close friend and colleague, Dr King, were comrades during a turbulent period in America's history. Even after Dr King was martyred, you passionately championed the noble dream that the two of you had shared, and you persevered in this battle for your convictions. I understand that you first met in 1958 when you were visiting Alabama, where Dr King lived.

HARDING: Yes. Several years before that time, I had completed my tour of duty as a draftee in the US Army. During that military service, when the Korean 'conflict' was coming to an end, I realized that, as a follower of Jesus, my conscience would not allow me to train myself to destroy other people whom my government defined as 'the enemy'.

It was in this developmental context that I began my doctoral studies in history at the University of Chicago, and it was there that I met a group of Mennonites. The Mennonites and other Christian groups such as the Quakers and the Church of the Brethren were known as peace churches in the United States. At their best, they tried to take seriously Jesus's teaching to 'love your enemies', and they endeavoured to live according to this guidance.

A group of Mennonites invited me to join them in exploring the possibility of creating an inclusive church community of black and white Christians. In the course of our work, some of us asked ourselves: 'What would we do if we were living in the South, where it is illegal and dangerous for blacks and whites to live and work together as sisters and brothers? Would we still try to live as we believe and honour our relationships with one another, even if we might get into serious trouble?'

In the fall of 1958, five of us – three whites and two blacks, all young men in our twenties and thirties (and likely with a touch of the daredevil in us) – decided to go south and try to find out. The five of us got into an old station wagon and promised ourselves that we would refuse to be separated, that we would try in every way to keep together as a family of brothers in Christ. 'Let's see what happens,' we agreed.

IKEDA: So, this was a major first step toward living your convictions. How courageous an act this must have been during that period. The stark nature of racial discrimination in a number of southern states was reported even in Japan.

HARDING: Following the historic US Supreme Court decision of 1954, which declared segregation to be unconstitutional, it was in 1955 that the Montgomery bus boycott, provoked by Rosa Parks's unjust arrest (see Conversation Seven), grew into a massive groundswell that spread throughout the South.

This was a time when, in many places in the South, numerous conflicts were erupting, and tensions were heightened. In 1956, the University of Alabama in Tuscaloosa admitted its first African-American student, but in the end, she was not permitted to attend because of violence on campus and in the streets of Tuscaloosa. The university's board of directors refused to reinstate her, despite a court order.

Then, in 1957, nine black students were refused entry into Little Rock Central High School in Arkansas. After much urging, President Dwight D. Eisenhower agreed to send federal troops to Little Rock to ensure the entry of the nine and their protection.

As the five of us travelled south, we decided that our first entry point into the southern experience would be in Arkansas. It was one year after that explosion of racial conflict surrounding the high school in Little Rock. Our first stop was to contact Daisy Bates, the local head of the National Association for the Advancement of Colored People and a key figure in helping the students who had integrated Little Rock Central High School. She and her husband published the local black newspaper.

We went to her house, and I will always remember her living room window, broken by a rock that had been thrown through it. The note accompanying the rock read, 'The next time there will be dynamite.' We were impressed by the courage of Mrs Bates and her husband, and their refusal to be intimidated.

After Little Rock, we continued on our journey, moving with some fear and trembling through Mississippi, the state with the worst record of terrorist violence against anyone who challenged the antihuman practices of segregation and white supremacy. With the assistance of courageous black and white supporters, we made it safely through Mississippi and stopped next in Alabama, in the southern part of the state, many miles from Montgomery, the state's capital.

We decided that we absolutely must try to see Dr King while we were in the state. Of course, in those days there were no cell phones. We looked up 'King' in the Montgomery phone book, and we reached Coretta Scott King, Martin's wife. Mrs King told us that her husband was recuperating from a stab wound he had recently received in an attack by a deranged person. Dr King had been on a book-signing tour in New York City when this happened. After being hospitalized in New York, he was at home but had been sent to bed by his doctor. Coretta warmly invited us to stop by, although she cautioned us that her husband might not feel well enough to see us. Despite the uncertainty, we decided to drive to Montgomery to King's home.

IKEDA: I can imagine how energetic and action-oriented you must have been in your younger days. And it was wonderful that Mrs King welcomed you with such warmth and understanding.

In 1995, we invited Mrs King to the Calabasas campus of SUA to talk on human rights. She was pleased to meet our Japanese study-abroad students from Soka Women's College, who had the unforgettable experience of coming into direct contact with a person who embodied the American human rights struggle.

I want young people, the future leaders of society, to take advantage of every opportunity to learn from their predecessors' courageous struggles. I sincerely hope that they will learn the spiritual lessons of that history and use them to build a better, more just society. I say this because young people will lead the way to a new era. Young people form the core of our Soka Gakkai International movement for peace, culture and education based on Buddhism. I want to see the youth take bold action in the interest of peace and human rights.

For those of us who are older, we have a responsibility to help open a path for the youth to accomplish these objectives. We have a mission to transmit the truth of history to them.

HARDING: When we arrived at Dr King's home, Mrs King expressed appreciation for us and our pilgrimage. She realized the danger we were courting by travelling around the South as a racially mixed group. So, she readily went into the bedroom to announce our arrival, and when she returned, she reported that Dr King was glad we had come, and that he wanted to meet with us for a little while.

Mrs King ushered us into the bedroom, where Dr King warmly greeted us in his pyjamas and robe. As we sat in chairs around his bed, he spoke of how glad he was to find out about our work and how much he respected the peace churches. He was heartened that our activities and his own shared a common thread – we all observed the principles and practices of non-violence and recognized the need for humane social change.

We spoke to Dr King about our activities in Chicago and the various adventures we had experienced on our road trip. With his wonderful sense of humour, he congratulated us for having survived Mississippi. The conversation lasted for a little more than an hour. As we rose to leave, Dr King spoke directly to me and my friend Ed Riddick, the other black man in our group: 'You men are part of the Mennonites, and so you know what we are trying to do here with non-violence. You understand this, and I think you all should find a way to come back down here and help us out.'

I am sure that Dr King spoke partially in jest, but he also seemed serious. However he meant it, his words had a powerful effect on me, and I never forgot them. Three years later, my wife and I accepted his invitation and moved from Chicago to the South to participate in the civil rights movement and reconnect with King and his family.

Humour's Essential Role

Ikeda: It seems that your meeting with Dr King was destined to have a decisive impact on your lives. A momentary encounter can sometimes decide the shape of one's entire future. For youth especially, each encounter is of critical importance. This is why I take my contacts with young people seriously and make each moment matter.

In any case, I now have a clearer sense of the serious conditions under which Dr King worked and the passion you and your friends had in your youth. So, following your move to the South, you grew closer to the King family.

Please tell me, what most impressed you the first time you met Dr King?

HARDING: What impressed me were his curiosity, creativity, courage and openness, and these were characteristics that continued to define him throughout his life. During that first Montgomery encounter, he was impressed that the five of us – two blacks and three whites – were travelling together as brothers. This was tremendously important to him.

One of his major goals was not simply to establish legal rights for black people but to go beyond that to create what he termed the 'beloved community', in which all people could rediscover a sense of our fundamental connectedness as human beings. What King and other spiritually grounded leaders in the movement were trying to teach was that our ultimate goal was to create a new America – an America where blacks and whites, as well as people of all colours, could come together to find common ground for the common good.

I was also impressed by Martin's great intellect and his enjoyment of ideas, as well as his adventurous spirit and love of a challenge. I think that it was these characteristics of Martin's that inspired his interest in us and enabled him to understand what we were doing. He understood that this country would not truly heal from its deep racial divisions unless more people were willing to reach across racial and class lines, even at great risk to themselves. He often used the motto 'We've got to organize goodness.'

We were touched by the fact that even though Martin was suffering from his wound, he still invited us into his bedroom, manifesting the tradition of hospitality so imbedded in southern black life. Another aspect that especially impressed me was Martin's wonderful sense of humour.

IKEDA: Thank you for sharing these precious memories. Each one is an infinitely priceless, historical testimony. The ultimate goal for Dr King and his colleagues was, as you said, the creation of a new America in which people of all colours and backgrounds could find common ground. This is another motivation that draws many Soka Gakkai International members in the United States to Buddhist practice.

Buddhism teaches that all people possess the Buddha nature and are deserving of the utmost respect. With this conviction in their hearts, people of diverse cultural backgrounds have marched forward together, arm in arm, in pursuit of peace, radiating their equal reverence for their own lives and the lives of others. This is the beautiful network of solidarity our members are building in American society.

The only way to fundamentally resolve the ethnic and national conflicts our world is facing is to return to the starting point of life itself and our shared humanity. We all desire peace and happiness, no matter the colour of our skin, the language we speak or our cultural heritage. Everything depends on how successful we are in nurturing and promoting an underlying empathy and spiritual unity as fellow human beings who all cherish our families and share the same human joys and sufferings.

You just mentioned Dr King's wonderful sense of humour, and I recall that he has been described as a person who loved to laugh.

HARDING: I think that Martin developed a tremendous sense of humour in the same way that many of his colleagues did, and that those who have lived through danger, oppression and great difficulties have. It is one way that we can rise above the tensions and traumas, and move forward – an engaging kind of humour that is clever and creative, not light or foolish.

This is a truth that people who have studied the human condition have identified. Humour and laughter help us be open to life and are what we sometimes need when we are overcome by tension and difficulty. Perhaps it is precisely the physical act of opening our mouths to laugh that is a powerful aspect of the healing process.

IKEDA: The well-known American poet Maya Angelou also recalled that Dr King was a man full of courage with a rich sense of humour:

> Dr King, in the face of the most horrid situations, the most cruel people, the most greedy and mean-spirited, he kept his spirit up, and quite often, with a wonderful smile.[1]

Ms Angelou also pointed out that Dr King's humour endeared him to people and made him more approachable.

Laughter and humour contain within them a powerful means of overcoming all manner of trials and tribulations by bringing people together and inspiring courage. They also have a wondrous capacity to provide relief and optimism to the anxious heart.

Mahatma Gandhi once famously said, 'If I had no sense of humour, I should long ago have committed suicide.'[2] Gandhi also was one who loved to laugh.

People are naturally drawn to cheerfulness and joy. No matter how noble a movement's ideals and philosophy, if its leaders become negative and uninspiring, or if the movement becomes inflexible and bureaucratic, it will fail to thrive. Dr King must have had a keen understanding of this.

HARDING: This brings to mind an interesting memory. One summer night in 1962, in the midst of an intense desegregation campaign in Albany, Georgia, Martin asked me to lead a group of black citizens in a demonstration at the city hall. The purpose of the demonstration was to protest the beating of a pregnant community leader by a police officer. We felt that the community had to have some public way to voice its anger and indignation or a dangerous and explosive situation would develop.

As a result of the public action, I was arrested and thrown into jail. This occurred in July 1962, just before my thirty-first birthday.

One or two days later, Martin, my wife and several others came to see me in jail. Martin stood there, looking at me through the prison bars, and said, 'Well, Vincent, I know it is your birthday, and we would have brought you a birthday cake, but Chief Pritchett probably would not have let us give it to you.'

It just so happened that there was an old comic strip that portrayed a character giving a prisoner a birthday cake with a metal file in it for sawing through the prison bars, allowing the prisoner to escape. So, Martin joked, 'We didn't think we could get away with it, so you'll have to wait until you get out to have your birthday cake.' This was typical – he loved to joke and tease people.

IKEDA: What an entertaining story. It conveys Dr King's warm, good-humoured nature.

My mentor also never forgot his sense of humour. In the turbulent, chaotic aftermath of World War II, many Japanese suffered from disease and poverty. After surviving two years of detainment under harsh conditions imposed by the military authorities, Mr Toda took a stand and dedicated himself completely to the common people, plunging himself into the task of building a peace movement based on Buddhist principles. He felt moved to help the distressed and suffering, no matter what it took. So, he put his entire heart and soul into encouraging them.

It would be impossible to measure how much each little humorous remark of his gave comfort and strength, chasing away the dark clouds, shining the bright light of hope on each person's heart. He once encouraged people in the depths of misery by saying:

> For what purpose were you born as human beings? This seems to be a simple question, but actually it is very difficult to answer. To be brief, you have come into this world to amuse yourselves. No matter where you are, you are there to enjoy your lives fully and have whatever fun you like at any time. That is the purpose of life . . . Sweet bean soup needs much sugar and a touch of salt in order to be really sweet. Likewise, you cannot realize what true happiness is unless there is a certain amount of hardship in your lives. In your case, there is more salt than sugar. How can anyone eat sweet bean soup that is salty?[3]

With this amusing and at the same time convincing explanation, he made us see that we were better off trying to enjoy life and helped us rouse our courage to face the harsh challenges of reality. Consequently, through our practice of Buddhism, we were victorious and created the lives we had hoped to live.

Today's Soka Gakkai was created by countless ordinary people, one after another, standing up jubilantly. My mentor was a rare leader who walked together with the people.

Harding: He was a great leader, wasn't he?

I have one more anecdote to share with you that illustrates Martin's humour. It took place in Memphis, Tennessee, the place where he engaged in his last campaign and was felled by an assassin's bullet. Some of my friends with him then said that they would let off steam by having pillow fights in their hotel rooms. Martin would join in, and they would all playfully beat one another with pillows, laughing wholeheartedly.

Andrew Young was the staff person probably closest to Martin at the time. On 4 April 1968, the last day of Martin's life, Andy had to be in a Memphis court most of the day, and when he returned to the hotel, Martin playfully grilled him on where he had been and why he hadn't notified anyone. 'You should know that you should at least give us a call,' he scolded. Then, with a big smile, he started pummelling Andy with a pillow, and Andy responded by grabbing another pillow and beating him back. It was a funny moment, and everyone was in stitches, eventually participating in the pillow fight as well.

The Dimensions of Courage

Ikeda: I can just imagine it.

People with conviction and resolve to fulfil their mission find their courage. They have a fearless fighting spirit. And courageous people are always light-hearted and cheerful.

Gandhi observed: 'Strength does not come from physical capacity. It comes from an indomitable will.'[4] Dr King embodies this statement. You seem to be saying that so many people were attracted to Dr King because of his extraordinary character and courage.

Harding: Martin's courage was displayed in various ways, and the courageous actions that are especially noteworthy seem to be concentrated in the last year of his life. He was, of course, aware that he was a target and could be shot and killed at any moment. The great evidence of his courage was his refusal to turn away from his commitment to the struggle. He would not allow the threat of death to stop him from being a public figure and champion of the causes that were so important in his life and for so many people.

In a talk I was giving not long ago to teenagers at a Denver middle school, I mentioned that King knew that he could well be killed if he continued to speak and act on his beliefs. But I didn't go into detail about it because I didn't think it was necessary. Afterward, one young man came right up to me as I was preparing to leave.

He said, 'Dr Harding, I have a question to ask you.'

I told him: 'Please ask. I love questions.'

He asked in a wonderfully youthful and challenging voice: 'I want to know this: If Dr King knew that he could be killed at any time, why didn't he just chill out for a while?'

I paused for a moment, trying to think of a good way to explain to the boy what courage and commitment are. Just then, up walked a young girl about the same age, and she made it absolutely unnecessary for me to say anything. She said to her young classmate: 'What do you mean "chill out?" He couldn't chill out – he had work to do.'

This summed it up well. Martin's courage came from his dedication to the work he felt was his to do on this Earth.

IKEDA: This explains it all, doesn't it? I can picture you in this conversation with the earnest young man and the wise young woman.

In Dr King's words: 'Courage faces fear and thereby masters it. Cowardice represses fear and is thereby mastered by it.'[5] Dr King stood up to the evils of society and was prepared to accept the consequences. His determined action ignited a roaring blaze of courage in people's hearts. The emergence of such an exceptional leader as Martin Luther King created the historical context and stage for a movement truly of the people, by the people and for the people.

The British historian Arnold Toynbee made an unforgettable observation about the requirements for leadership. He said in effect that the absolutely indispensable conditions for successful leadership are courage and confidence, as well as the ability to inspire these sentiments in the people's hearts.

Toynbee added that it is also, of course, necessary for leaders and the people they lead to be linked by a common cause that appeals to the heart. If the appeal is sufficiently strong, leaders can inspire people to follow them into any venture, no matter how seemingly impossible.[6]

Courage is a value that is frequently emphasized in Buddhism. In the Lotus Sutra, which represents the essence of Mahayana Buddhism, courage is affirmed in expressions such as 'They have exerted themselves bravely and vigorously'[7] and 'the power of the buddhas that has the lion's ferocity'.[8] We Soka Gakkai members have come this far by fearlessly embracing this spirit.

Without courage, we cannot create a just world. In addition, cowardliness may ultimately result in aiding and abetting the forces of evil. As my mentor often said, 'It can be hard to summon compassion, but courage can take the place of compassion.'

HARDING: At the same time, my friend, it is important for us to remember that it was often the courage and determination of the ordinary people that helped to inspire King to his best leadership. This was certainly the case in Montgomery, where he first arrived in 1954 as a twenty-five-year-old graduate student and found a community already determined to work for change. People like Mrs Parks (see Conversation Seven) helped Martin to discover his capacity for leadership, helped him to develop his courage.

I have always felt that Martin's life could be summed up in these four Cs: courage, commitment, creativity and compassion. These were at the heart of his being.

One of his greatest acts of courage was his willingness to come out publicly against the Vietnam War and to raise serious doubts about not just the war but about America's approach to the world (see Conversation Eleven). You may ask why such courage was necessary. One reason is that President Lyndon B. Johnson had identified himself completely with the war and the effort to win. At the same time, he also considered himself a friend of the black freedom movement. Many of the people in the movement did perceive Johnson that way. Therefore, for King to oppose the war meant that he was, in a way, opposing the president of the United States, an important ally in the movement for civil rights. This was a decision that King had to make.[9]

IKEDA: The flames of the fifteen-year-long Vietnam War enveloped and devastated the lives of too many people. It must have been dangerous to advocate against the war at that time. I can imagine the anguish Dr King must have suffered in making his decision. This is an important issue in Dr King's life as well as in the civil rights movement, so I want to revisit this subject (see Conversation Eleven).

CONVERSATION FIVE

On Encouragement

IKEDA: As expressed in the immortal wisdom of Dr King, 'Life's most persistent and urgent question is, What are you doing for others?'[1] Your response to the noble sentiment expressed in this question has been to spend your entire life courageously fighting for a world that honours human dignity and protects human rights. Our dialogue, in which we've been discussing your personal experiences with Dr King during your youth, has already drawn an enthusiastic response from our readers.[2]

Let me ask about your memories of another of your closest companions, your late partner in the civil rights struggle and beloved wife, Rosemarie. How did you meet her?

HARDING: I first met Rosemarie in Chicago, where she grew up, around the time that I joined the Mennonite church community. It was in 1959, when I was invited to be one of the speakers at a Mennonite conference on race. It turned out that she was also on the programme.

People had been telling me about Rosemarie before then, that I should meet her, and so, during the conference, when the opportunity arose, I summoned up my courage and introduced myself to her. I still remember what she was wearing that day. She always was a sharp dresser. We promised to stay in touch after that. That's how our relationship began – with a discussion about problems of racial discrimination.

At that time, Rosemarie was already teaching third grade at a public elementary school, and I was just finishing my doctoral coursework and beginning to work on my dissertation. As we grew to know each other better, I discovered that she held a deep commitment to the Mennonite philosophy of creating a peaceful world, and we talked more and more about events in the South. I also remember that we attended a talk by Dr King in Chicago together.

IKEDA: So you met while participating in various peace and human rights activities and discovered that you were kindred spirits who shared the same noble ideals. Rosemarie was a superb leader who fought on the front lines of the civil rights movement. Can you share anything that she said to you that remains engraved upon your heart?

HARDING: Shortly after we married, I attended a conference where I was one of the speakers. After the conference, when we returned to our lodging, Rosemarie told me:

> Vincent, you know you are very good at analysing situations. And you are very good at telling people what more they need to do beyond what they are currently doing and what they aren't doing very well. You are very good at those kinds of things, but I think that what people need more than anything else is encouragement – encouragement to be better than they are. Vincent, I think that you can do a very good job at that.

In a profound sense, Rosemarie helped me to discover my deepest calling. The older I become, the more I realize how true her words were.

IKEDA: What priceless words of wisdom. And it was marvellous the way you took her precious advice to heart and implemented it. Your activities and mission today, it seems to me, remain connected with your wife.

As Rosemarie pointed out, encouragement is what gives people understanding and hope to generate the strength to move forward with vigour and positivity. Encouragement is also fundamental in education, isn't it?

Nichiren,[3] whose teachings we in the Soka Gakkai International follow, wrote, 'Teaching another something is the same as oiling the wheels of a cart so that they turn even though it is heavy, or as floating a boat on water so that it moves ahead easily.'[4] Encouragement is indeed the special ingredient that enables a person to move ahead with confidence and peace of mind. Our Soka Gakkai International movement, based on the Buddhist philosophy of life, offers infinite encouragement to light the flame of exceptional courage in people's hearts.

HARDING: Rosemarie taught me that encouragement is what people need, and that I am capable of providing it. Ever since then, I have tried to offer it in a variety of ways in every context in which I have found myself.

It is not always clear what will encourage someone. However, it is good to remind people that each of us already possesses an enormous capacity to live our most cherished hopes and dreams, and to achieve our highest potential. I think that people are helped when I let them know that I see their potential, and that I believe they are capable of achieving it. I let them know that I believe they can discover and actualize this best self.

IKEDA: This is the essence of humane, ethical education. Nichiren teaches, 'One experiences [great Joy] when one understands for the first time that one's mind from the very beginning has been the Buddha.'[5] Nothing can surpass the joy of being awakened to one's sublime state of life. In any case, encouragement helps open the door to people's infinite potential and inspires them to bring their talents into full flower.

So many people have been positively influenced and encouraged by you and your wife to stand up fearlessly and commit themselves to a life of mission. I can visualize all these individuals, advancing proudly with heads held high.

I am reminded of my December 2009 meeting with former president Gorbachev, during which we remembered his late wife, Raisa. In her memoirs, Mrs Gorbachev wrote:

> My fervent wish is that somehow my husband could remain just as he was as a young man, when I first met him. I want him to be courageous, strong, and kind-hearted. I want him to be able to sing the songs he loves, recite his favorite poetry, and laugh with gay abandon, as he has always done.

When I reminded Mr Gorbachev of this, he smiled and said:

> Our lives have been full of dramatic events. Russia, our Motherland, has also endured many bitter hardships. My late wife, Raisa, knew all of this firsthand, and she took every problem to heart as if it were her own and lived through and overcame it.

You must have similar recollections. I am sure that your late wife is watching over you, proud of the way you have continued your noble struggle with the same ideals and passion of your youth, encouraging many people in the course of your journey.

HARDING: You are so kind.

IKEDA: How magnificent is a human being! Buddhism teaches that within every person there exists infinite potential. Encouragement elicits the virtuous traits of hope, courage and compassion in people's lives.

The Lotus Sutra teaches us to 'open the door of buddha wisdom to all living beings . . . awaken living beings to the buddha wisdom [and] cause living beings to enter the path of buddha wisdom'.[6] It teaches that the purpose of Buddhism is to open and reveal the supreme Buddha wisdom inherent in all people and awaken and inspire them to enter the path leading to the supreme way of living as explained by Buddhism.

No matter what trials we encounter, we can call forth unlimited wisdom and strength to overcome them with bravery and courage. Faith provides the basis for this, and the power of encouragement from one's peers is the driving force behind the strength to live with this faith.

I can understand how your dear wife's advice precipitated a major awakening in your life. The words of perceptive women contain deep life wisdom and keen insight into reality.

Please share some of your thoughts on raising your children. At the peak of your intense struggles in the civil rights movement, how did you and your wife educate your children?

HARDING: Well, our daughter, Rachel, was born a little over a year after we moved to the South. One of my most vivid memories is how we took Rachel along with us as often as possible as we travelled all over the South. We were driving a little black Ford

Falcon then, and we took out the backseat and secured a baby crib there so that she could join us as a passenger in all our travels. That was how we dealt with the child-raising issue then. We felt instinctively that we wanted Rachel to experience what we were experiencing, and that we needed to have her with us as a part of what we were doing.

The Living Model of Our Own Lives

IKEDA: That's a heart-warming story. In our dialogue,[7] Dr Elise Boulding, the eminent peace scholar, shared a similar experience. She and her husband were both peace activists, and as much as possible they took their children along to peace movement activities. Dr Boulding maintained that peace education begins in the family. The family is an excellent environment for nurturing in a person a heart of empathy and compassion, the courage to act on behalf of justice and the wisdom to create peace in one's community.

In the Soka Gakkai, many young couples bring their children along with them to discussions, peace movement activities and study groups, where the parents are learning about the life-affirming principles of Buddhism. By observing their parents devoting themselves to benefitting others and society, the children learn a great deal in an unforced, natural way.

The Buddhist scriptures emphasize the important role of the persons who uphold and transmit the Buddhist teachings. Without them, it is as if 'there were only wooden or stone statues garbed in priests' robes and carrying begging bowls'.[8]

A major issue for any system of thought or faith is how to transmit its ideas to future generations. The only way for parents to transmit philosophy and faith principles to their children is to provide them, first of all, with the living model of their own lives. Children learn what is important in life through the earnest examples of their parents.

The same goes for nurturing and educating youth in general. Most important is the way that adults think, speak and act.

When we speak of the history of the civil rights movement in the 1950s and 1960s, we must not overlook the contribution of women. One outstanding woman, Ella Jo Baker, encouraged and guided many youth in those days. She was a distinguished leader who served as the executive director of the Southern Christian Leadership Conference.

HARDING: Before we discuss Ella Baker, please let me provide a brief description of the Southern Christian Leadership Conference. Several years after the Montgomery bus boycott, King decided, with the encouragement of people in the South as well as other parts of the country who knew him and what he was doing, to form the Southern Christian Leadership Conference. The conference grew to be one of the best-known organizations among the southern freedom groups.

Originally, the Southern Christian Leadership Conference was made up of Martin's preacher friends interested in being active in social change efforts in a positive way. Most of them were black Baptist preachers and, therefore, mostly men.

Some of King's friends in the movement in the North, especially New York, encouraged him and other leaders of the organization to hire a director. None of the preachers could give full-time guidance to the organization. This led to the hiring of a magnificent woman for the job. Her name was Ella Josephine Baker. The preachers had a difficult time dealing with such a strong, outspoken black woman. That is a whole story in itself!

IKEDA: Oh, I see! The outspoken opinions of women of this calibre do indeed ring with truth.

Incidentally, several years ago I gave a speech in which I introduced the story of Ella Baker's life to a gathering of Soka Gakkai women. Ella Baker was a fearless woman who, beginning before World War II, dedicated her life to the struggle for human rights. When she became the director of the Southern Christian Leadership Conference, she was already in her mid-fifties, but she was still very active.

I understand that Baker toured the entire south and nurtured new talent for the movement. She was exceptionally effective in garnering the trust and respect of the younger generation. Rosa Parks was one of the people who gathered around Ella Baker and was influenced by her.

HARDING: It was wonderful how Ella Baker took the opportunity to contact so many youth through her position at the Southern Christian Leadership Conference. When young people began their 'sit-ins', King and the Southern Christian Leadership Conference dreamed of making them a youth division within their movement. However, when Ella Baker saw the energy, courage and potential of these young people, she encouraged them to form their own organization rather than become an arm of an existing one, merely assisting with someone else's agenda. So, they formed the Student Nonviolent Coordinating Committee, and Ella Baker became their advisor and major encourager.

IKEDA: Ella Baker had an absolute, unwavering trust in the youth, and that's why they put their trust in her. When people criticized her for putting too much confidence in young people, she defended them, saying that 'they were entitled to youthful mistakes'.[9] She had a big, big heart.

When young people believe that people are counting on them and are putting their trust in them, they can muster enormous power. People in leadership positions must always bear this in mind. This theme of trust in youth reminds me of Sir Joseph Rotblat, the British physicist active as the president and subsequently president emeritus of the Pugwash Conferences on Science and World Affairs. He was still active in the peace movement in his nineties, working with an assistant sixty years his junior.

In his dialogues with me, Sir Joseph emphasized respect for the energy and motivation of the young. Of his young assistant, he said, 'We are like brothers, encouraging each other and working together as colleagues.'[10]

Professor Rotblat dedicated himself to nurturing the next generation of young scientists and was responsible for founding the Student/Young Pugwash group. I will never forget the earnestness in his voice when he told me, 'We must devote all our efforts to nurture the up-and-coming generation so that they can survive and build a world that is much better than the one we are leaving them.'[11]

Any organization that values the youth and strives to help them realize their unlimited potential will never reach a dead end or be at a loss for ideas. It will continue growing and moving forward. This is a lesson I learned from my mentor, who treasured and placed his trust in young people.

The Leader As Peacemaker

Harding: The radicalism of the youth in the Student Nonviolent Coordinating Committee challenged the Southern Christian Leadership Conference to become a better organization. One of the major points of contention was how to organize people. The Southern Christian Leadership Conference grew out of the black ministerial tradition, which was essentially a patriarchal model for organizing around a charismatic leader.

On the other hand, the young people, under the influence of Ella Baker, developed the idea and practice of *participatory democracy*. This is a philosophy of governance in which the responsibilities of leadership are shared widely, the leadership capacities of all encouraged and developed. King acknowledged the importance of this approach, but he was a child of the black church, which is a patriarchal institution, like almost all traditional churches.

Another area of disagreement among some of the youth was the issue of the efficacy of non-violence. The practice of non-violence requires much patience, a quality that youth often have in short supply. Also, many of these were young Americans who believed in the principle of an eye for an eye and a tooth for a tooth, which expressed the American cultural worldview. These young people had to re-educate and remake themselves into non-violent warriors. Not unlike other movements growing out of a democratic context, the dynamics of this process were complex, and things did not always go as smoothly as it may have appeared from the outside.

As the movement took root, many local organizations emerged in the metropolitan as well as rural areas. They each had their own emphasis and focus, and there was some envy among these groups concerning the national and international attention focused on King.

At heart, Martin was a superb peacemaker, and so he was always trying to collaborate with these groups. But in many instances, the groups were engaged in bitter conflicts among themselves. So, he had to play the role of peacemaker to create a sense of unity among his fellow soldiers in the movement.

IKEDA: This is one of the realities of human society in general, isn't it? In the East, we have a cautionary analogy about parasites in the lion's body: The mighty lion, the king of beasts, may be destroyed by worms that eat him from the inside. Though an organization may be invincible against its external enemies, its downfall may come through discord and confusion within. No matter how strong an organization may seem, without constant vigilance, it may collapse from within.

Dr King had to deal with disharmony and other problems within the movement at the same time that he was battling external forces intent on crushing the civil rights movement.

HARDING: One point that became clear by the beginning of the 1960s was that the federal government and many of the state governments were constantly scheming to infiltrate the civil rights movement.[12] King and his colleagues were aware of this and accepted it as one aspect of engaging in a democratic social movement to change the status quo.

It seemed to me that Martin was guided in every situation by a spirit of non-violence, and he refused to let fear of infiltrators dominate his thinking. It was a spirit that was constantly prompting us to figure out how to help these infiltrators who were morally in trouble. I am sure he faced the conflict that those responsible for the health and well-being of an organization or institution feel when they want to protect their group without descending to the same level as the enemies who want to destroy it.

This is similar to what we are facing in the United States today. We are grappling with the issue of security – what it means to be secure and how to achieve it, also whether we can abide someone else's security being sacrificed in the process. This is the conflict that we are struggling to clarify.

In any case, toward the end, Martin was fairly sure that there were at least one or two people within the organization who had suspicious motivations. But, of course, Martin was at heart a minister. This led him to always approach people with compassion and the desire to understand how to heal their personal wounds, even though they might be trying to wound the organization.

IKEDA: This was part of Dr King's appeal, wasn't it? When there were differences of opinion about strategy and the principles of the movement, how were they resolved?

NG: King was always growing in his understanding of :t resolution and how to find solutions to differences of ons. In many instances, he would ask the people with the disagreements to argue their cases, and he would listen to their ideas and conclusions.

In a couple of cases to which I was privy, after he listened carefully to the arguments of each side, Martin left the room for a time. When he returned, he shared with everyone what he believed should be done. This was the final decision. It was not the most democratic means of decision-making, but it was the nature and process of an organization based on charismatic leadership.

IKEDA: You are probably right.

Every people's movement needs responsible leadership – leaders with the capacity to bring together the thoughts and opinions of the parties involved and then make the courageous decisions necessary to advance their cause. It's the only way to achieve clear-cut victory in difficult struggles.

There is bound to be some degree of friction in every movement. Indeed, in a new, popular movement, plotting inspired by envy and malice is bound to occur, and the movement is likely to be misunderstood. This was true with the Soka Gakkai International as well.

The way to overcome these challenges is for leaders to work together in harmony and, while summoning greater strength than that of opposing forces, continue to engage in their own vibrant growth and personal development. Following the example of Dr King's constant striving toward personal growth and development, leaders must always seek to understand the people's perspective and walk humbly with them. Leaders must never become arrogant or self-important and forget that their role is to represent and serve the people.

CONVERSATION SIX

Influential Encounters

IKEDA: A positive family environment can be a crucible for character building. In addition, positive social encounters can be a source of inspiration for realizing our full potential.

I want to explore the influences that were important for Dr King and especially to shed light on the kind of people Dr King's parents were and the influential encounters he had with people in his youth.

Dr King was born on 15 January 1929, in Atlanta, the son of Martin Luther King Sr, a Baptist minister, and his wife, Alberta. Did you ever meet Dr King's parents?

HARDING: I knew both his parents. It is important to realize that his mother, Mrs Alberta Williams King, was the daughter of the minister of Ebenezer Baptist Church. As she grew up, she became a musician in the church, playing the piano and organ. She had a long history in the congregation. This is important in understanding just how embedded her son was in the life of the congregation.

IKEDA: He grew up observing his mother devote herself to the service of others. A mother's example is imprinted on a child's mind and influences his or her entire life. The way Dr King felt about the church is clear from his comment "The church has always been a second home for me.'[1]

He also expressed appreciation for his mother, who, he said, 'instilled a sense of self-respect in all of her children'.[2] As a child, he learned at his mother's knee all about the history of black people in America. She explained why black people were in a position of such inequality, and she would tell her son, 'You are as good as anyone.'[3]

These kind words of motherly love and confidence surely provided her son powerful emotional support. What is great about motherhood is its fiercely courageous spirit, which valiantly protects and nurtures life, even in the face of life's worst storms.

HARDING: Dr King's mother was obviously very proud of him. I talked with her a number of times. I especially remember when I met with her after the assassination, when we were beginning to establish the King Memorial Library. She had carefully stored years and years of church bulletins, and she pulled out boxes and boxes of them from under her bed for us.

As you may know, not long after Martin's assassination, she was killed by a deranged man. He came into the church and shot her as she was sitting at the organ.

IKEDA: It's a terrible tragedy, isn't it? She was a noble martyr who had encouraged many. Her achievements will endure forever, alongside those of her son. It was a shame she didn't live for many more years.

HARDING: It was a great pity. She was a kind and calm person and had a solid and focused way about her. It's important to know that after she gave birth to Martin, her own mother, Jennie Williams, helped her to raise the children. So, Alberta King's mother – Martin's grandmother – was also an important presence in his life.

I have read a lot of research that suggests that maternal grandmothers have a profound influence on the development of their grandchildren. This certainly seems to be borne out in the lives of many of the people I've worked with, especially those engaged in social change.

So, Grandmother Williams was important to King. From everything I know about their relationship, she encouraged him to think of himself as having the capacity to become a great leader.

IKEDA: Dr King was raised by two outstanding women who showered him with love and encouragement, and this is undoubtedly why he developed into such an influential leader.

This reminds me of the words of one of my friends, the well-known Argentine champion of human rights Adolfo Pérez Esquivel. In 2001, at a meeting held in the United States, Dr Esquivel was one of five Nobel Peace Prize laureates in attendance. The conference moderator asked each one to answer the question, 'Who is the hero who has had the most profound meaning in your life?' The responses included President George Washington, Prime Minister Winston Churchill, playwright William Shakespeare, and the scientist Madame Curie. When it was Esquivel's turn, he proudly answered, 'My hero is my grandmother.' She was a wise indigenous woman.

Dr Esquivel was three when he lost his mother, and so he was raised by his maternal grandmother. His grandmother had endured many hardships growing up and had been unable to attend school. However, she had an uncanny insight into human character. She would give Dr Esquivel accurate advice about the people he knew, saying, 'That's a good person – he knows how to see you and hear you.' Or, of another person she would say: 'Watch out for him. He doesn't look at things straight on. He's ready to claw you at any moment.'[4]

Dr Esquivel told me, with a heart filled with profound appreciation for his grandmother and all the precious people who live ordinary yet exemplary lives of service to society, that he had proclaimed her his hero.

HARDING: My interest in maternal grandmothers began perhaps fifteen years ago when Rosemarie and I led a summer seminar at the Iliff School of Theology. We asked the participants to remember who had encouraged them to take the path of creating social change. We noticed that, almost without exception, they said that their maternal grandmothers had been important in encouraging them, in believing in them, and in letting them know that they were on the right path. Of course, there are always exceptions, but we discovered that the common experience was of maternal grandmothers being the most important in encouraging the youth.

IKEDA: That's a valuable testimony to the important influence that a grandfather's or grandmother's rich experience can have on a child's development. However, in contemporary society, because of changes in family structure and lifestyle, children have few opportunities to learn the precious wisdom and understanding of life that grandparents can impart. This is regrettable.

In the Soka Gakkai, we have many community activities attended by members of all ages. Our elderly members make these occasions to nurture our youth with care and compassion. In this way, young people can learn and benefit from their elders' rich fund of experience and wisdom, an important educational resource. The older members, in turn, are reinvigorated by contact with the young and also learn many new things.

Moving on, let me ask you about Dr King's father, who followed in the footsteps of his father-in-law to become a minister. Dr King once said, 'I have rarely ever met a person more fearless and courageous than my father . . .'[5]

Harding: King often spoke of his father's courage and fearlessness. In the black community, prior to the civil rights movement, the role of ministers was to speak their minds and work for change because they were essentially supported economically by the black community, whereas teachers and people in other occupations, who considered themselves much more vulnerable to white power, could not express their ideas freely and had to circumscribe their activities for fear of losing their jobs.

So, King's father had the opportunity to be more independent and bold in his role as a minister. Even though many pastors chose not to take any risks, it was clear that Martin Luther King Sr had decided to speak out courageously for what he believed.

What's the Purpose of Education?

Ikeda: A father's courage is passed down to his children. There is a well-known story about Dr King as a boy riding in a car with his father. A policeman stopped them and, speaking to Dr King's father in an insulting, paternalistic manner, even going so far as to call him 'boy', demanded to see his driver's licence. The older King pointed to his son and fearlessly retorted: 'This is a boy. I'm a man, and until you call me one, I will not listen to you.'[6] The policeman was at a loss for a response to the father's dignified, dauntless manner and so left as quickly as he could.

In an era when most people responded to the terrible wall of racial discrimination by suffering in silence, King's father showed great strength. It is not difficult to imagine how his father's courage nurtured a resolute spirit of justice in King's young heart.

HARDING: One point I want to mention in relation to King's father is that he was not necessarily the best model for Martin in terms of leadership style, given that he was part of the traditional black church. That is to say, by and large, the black church was not a democratic institution. It was a patriarchal one, and King had to wrestle with this and develop his own spirit and his own understanding of the kind of organization and the kind of country that he felt we must create.

IKEDA: Dr King also resisted the pressure of family members who hoped that he would become a minister like his father.

HARDING: When King first went to college, he wasn't sure whether he wanted to follow the path of his father and become a pastor. But he knew that he could not embrace his father's conservative theology and biblical literalism.

IKEDA: Dr King's view about entering the ministry changed as a result of his encounters with some of the professors at Morehouse College, didn't it? I have heard that he was profoundly influenced by the college president, Benjamin Elijah Mays, a leading scholar in the philosophy of black liberation.

HARDING: To provide some background, I want to make several important points about President Mays. One is that Mays had been a minister for many years before he entered the University of Chicago to study religion and sociology, and so he had successfully combined a life of scholarship and religious service.

Mays was also a master rhetorician. He had a magnificent command of language and the spoken word. In those days, all Morehouse College students were required to attend chapel service three times a week. At least one of those days was set aside for President Mays to talk with the all-male student body.

Central to his discussions with the students was his belief in their future role as leaders. This was one of his major themes – he told them they were preparing to be leaders not only of the black community but of the nation and the world. This was a powerful message to deliver during the 1940s and 1950s.

President Mays made a point of inviting people with broad experience and various racial backgrounds to the campus to speak to the students at the chapel assemblies. He became known as an inspiring leader who expanded the students' world and helped them to see that their education was not simply about preparing for a job but about becoming more fully human. All of these things about Mays impressed and attracted King.

IKEDA: Toda taught that meeting distinguished, talented people provides the best education for young people. Accordingly, I invite prominent leaders, artists and intellectuals from all over the world to the Soka schools and Soka University, and each encounter is a living education for the students.

President Mays described his university's mission in these terms:

> It is not sufficient for Morehouse College to produce clever graduates, men fluent in speech and able to argue their way through; but rather honest men who can be trusted in public and private life – men who are sensitive to the wrongs, the sufferings, and the injustices of society and who are willing to accept responsibility for correcting these ills.[7]

President Mays's statement shines with the light of truth, addressing with crystalline radiance the important question, 'What is the purpose of education?' When young people awaken to the real purpose of education, they can find a sense of mission and purpose, and their lives can glow with vitality and a powerful motivation. Their budding talents flourish rapidly, and their minds are set ablaze with a passion to seek truth. Dr King's encounter with President Mays represented the dawn of a new awareness in his life.

HARDING: President Mays was well respected in white and black educational and religious circles. He also published an important sociological work.[8] All of these factors made Mays attractive to King.

Perhaps most important, President Mays, as a scholar and a minister, had forged a path balancing a life of scholarship and one of religious calling. This was significant and powerful for King.

IKEDA: Dr King aspired to become a minister when he was in his fourth year at Morehouse College. After graduation, he studied at Crozer Theological Seminary in Pennsylvania, then did his doctorate at the Boston University School of Theology. During this period in King's life, were there other significant and enlightening encounters for him?

HARDING: Many of the characteristics that I mentioned of President Mays also match Dr Howard Thurman of Boston University. Dr Thurman was a spiritual and intellectual hero to many people in the black community. Parenthetically, Dr Thurman was a friend of Martin's father from their days as students at Morehouse.

Over the years, Dr Thurman became a public figure and visited black churches, black schools and black retreat centres on regular speaking tours. In those days, this was a common practice. Through these events, he shared his message with a wide audience. Dr Thurman was another great black orator who inspired and uplifted his audiences.

IKEDA: Dr Harold Case, Boston University president at that time, invited Thurman to become dean of the university's Marsh Chapel.

Incidentally, I had the opportunity to meet with Victor Kazanjian, Wellesley College's dean of International Education and Religious and Spiritual Life, who is Case's grandson. Kazanjian is an intellectual leader who passionately believes that education can change the world.

In the course of our conversation, the professor mentioned the friendship between President Case and Dr Thurman, and recalled that it also influenced him. In 1953, Dr Thurman assumed the position of dean of the chapel. He became the first black person to hold such a position in a major, long-established, predominantly white university. President Case's firm decision to welcome Dr Thurman as dean – in the face of widespread, irrational opposition – has been hailed as a decision of national importance. So, we can see how Dr King would have been influenced by Thurman.

Awakening the Adversary

Harding: Regarding Dr Thurman's influence on King, it was significant that in the 1930s, Dr Thurman and his wife travelled to India, where they had the valuable experience of meeting with Mahatma Gandhi. At that time, King was still a small child, but it was of some consequence that one of the first places that Dr and Mrs Thurman visited after their return from India was the King home.

Ikeda: This is a significant fact.

Harding: Dr Thurman believed instinctively that Gandhi's movement, especially its courageous non-violence, had a message for the black community in the United States. Even though it wasn't until King entered the seminary that he began to grasp the significance of this message, I think King never forgot that Thurman had met with Gandhi, face to face, and had discussed the situation in India and in the United States, how they were related.

Dr Thurman, like Mays, had always believed that religion and working for a just and compassionate world were two sides of the same coin and not separate in any way. This, I believe, was partly why Thurman had such an important influence on King.

IKEDA: When Dr Thurman travelled to India and met with Gandhi, he asked, among other things, for Gandhi's advice on advancing the non-violent movement in the United States. Gandhi responded, 'It may be through the Negroes that the unadulterated message of non-violence will be delivered to the world.'[9] Gandhi's words were prophetic and, in a way, reflected his most cherished hope for the future of humankind. They surely must have given Dr Thurman cause for deep contemplation.

Approximately twenty years later, under the leadership of Dr Thurman's student, Dr King, Gandhi's concept of non-violence became central to the movement for human rights and a powerful force in American society. I am moved by the passing of this baton – this commitment to the spirit of non-violence, championed by Gandhi – to a new generation in America.

HARDING: One of the ways in which black people in the United States became open to the larger world was through independent black newspapers, which could be found in black households, black barbershops, black churches and anywhere that black people congregated. These newspapers gave far, far more attention to Gandhi than any mainstream white newspapers. This was undoubtedly because he was a man of colour challenging the white, Western power structure that dominated much of the world. Another reason was that Gandhi's movement had a spiritual basis.

IKEDA: It's thought-provoking that a wide audience of ordinary people was exposed to the spirit of Gandhi through newspapers. Gandhi utilized newspapers to spread his message in India and in fact published his own newspaper, *Young India*, through which he instilled in Indian society his spirit of non-violence.

Newspapers wield enormous power. When my mentor's business was in dire straits, he and I formulated the vision for the *Seikyo Shimbun*, our organization's newspaper. It is amazing to think that the *Seikyo Shimbun*, which we dreamed into being so long ago, celebrates its sixtieth anniversary in 2011.

Dr King's perspective was transformed when he absorbed the significance of Gandhi's Salt March and his countless fasts, launched in protest to British rule. Before Dr King encountered Gandhi's philosophy, he had thought that Jesus's message of loving one's enemies was an individual ethic applicable only to interpersonal relationships. He had regarded the power of love as ineffectual in resolving social problems. King thought, for example, that a more realistic strategy of resistance was required in dealing with cruel, inhuman adversaries such as the Nazis or in resolving racial and ethnic conflicts.

However, studying Gandhi's actions radically changed King's thinking. As King explained:

> Gandhi was probably the first person in history to lift the love ethic of Jesus above mere interaction between individuals to a powerful and effective social force on a large scale. Love, for Gandhi, was a potent instrument for social and collective transformation. It was in this Gandhian emphasis on love and nonviolence that I discovered the method for social reform that I had been seeking for so many months.[10]

Dr King came to believe that love and non-violence were the only realistic and moral weapons of use in fighting for freedom. As you mentioned earlier, religion and the movement for justice became closely interconnected.

The dictum to love one's enemy is often interpreted as an instruction to not speak out against the enemy. However, this was not Dr King's understanding, was it?

HARDING: King knew that one of the critical aspects of the teaching to love one's enemy is the desire to not only free oneself from the hardships and struggles imposed by the enemy but, at the same time, to hope that the enemy has an opportunity to break out of the trap he or she has created for him- or herself. Essentially, this is compassion.

It is through compassion that we understand that an important part of our purpose in this world is to help others by whatever means possible – and assist our enemies in recovering from their illness and suffering. Our childish understanding of love is inadequate to grasp the depth of what Jesus and Gandhi were talking about.

IKEDA: On this point, Gandhi said:

> Satyagraha proceeds on the active principle of Love which says, 'Love those that despitefully use you. It is easy for you to love your friends. But I say unto you, love your enemies.'[11]

Indeed, those inspired by genuine love and compassion never avoid moral struggle or yield to the forces of evil.

Non-violent action is the struggle to elicit virtue and an awakening in the heart of the adversary. By transforming one's spiritual state, one also transforms one's opponent and society as a whole. It is, essentially, the struggle to save one's opponent. This resonates profoundly with our Buddhist movement's philosophy of human revolution.

HARDING: I can see that. It takes a mature understanding of both life and love to truly comprehend the intentions of mature individuals such as Gandhi, King, Thurman and Mordecai Johnson, president of Howard University and the one from whom King actually first learned about Gandhi's beliefs. Their concept of love was completely different from the popular notion represented in words such as 'My dear sweetheart, I think you're wonderful, you're beautiful.'

I remember Martin used to say: 'We're not called upon to *like* the enemy. We're called upon to *love* the enemy.'

Even in our personal relationships, we don't recognize sufficiently that to love is to seek the best for the other. Love is not a means of controlling the other or seeking what we want from the other. It means helping the other find out who he or she is meant to be. Love is also enabling the enemy to find out who they really are.

IKEDA: The Lotus Sutra provides, through Bodhisattva Never Disparaging's example, a model for how the faithful should live. Bodhisattva Never Disparaging, who, as his name suggests, never scorned or ridiculed others, was a seeker of the Way who appeared long after the death of Awesome Sound King Buddha. This was a period in which the true teachings of the Buddha were in decline, a time of rampant discrimination and violence in society. In such an age, Bodhisattva Never Disparaging told the many people he met, 'I have profound reverence for you',[12] and taught that the precious life condition of Buddhahood was inherent in every person. But the arrogant, conceited people he lived among pelted him with verbal abuse and slurs, beat him with sticks and staves, and threw rocks and tiles at him.

Nevertheless, Bodhisattva Never Disparaging refused to be intimidated. Wisely avoiding the violence of his opponents, he continued to declare, 'I have profound reverence for you', and carried on his practice. The bodhisattva continued to believe and spread the teaching that even within those who persecute, there abides the Buddha nature, the highest possible state of life. He demonstrated this essence of the Lotus Sutra in his life and religious practice.

Buddhism teaches: 'If one befriends another person but lacks the mercy to correct him, one is in fact his enemy',[13] and 'One who rids the offender of evil is acting as his parent.'[14] If you care about your adversary, you must correct his wrong thoughts and doings in order to prevent his unhappiness or misfortune. It is in this sense that I understand your description of the principle of love and non-violence.

HARDING: I find your perspective interesting. The direction that King began to move in was based on a combination of the beliefs of Gandhi and Jesus Christ. It clarified the goal of the struggle, even in the midst of injustice and oppression. That is to say, the goal of the struggle is not simply to eliminate injustice and oppression but to create a new reality. This is the intent of the principle of non-violence and the teachings of Jesus Christ.

As I mentioned previously (see Conversation Four), King eventually began to speak of these ideas in terms of how we must create the 'beloved community'. By this, he meant that the ultimate goal of the non-violent warrior is to create a situation in which enemies can become brothers and sisters, and new relationships are established.

CONVERSATION SEVEN

The Expansion of Democracy

IKEDA: Life is a drama. In the course of this drama, defining moments, pivotal events and crucial encounters occur that affect the course of one's entire life. After Dr King finished graduate school at Boston University, he took a position as pastor in Montgomery, Alabama. It was 1954, and Dr King was twenty-five.

Dr King's return, with his wife, Coretta, to the South, the area suffering the worst racial discrimination in the entire country, resulted in his taking leadership of the Montgomery bus boycott movement.

HARDING: And the catalyst for this historic movement was Rosa Parks, an ordinary woman who had been working for racial justice for many years and was active in the National Association for the Advancement of Colored People and the Women's Political Council, the black women's political advocacy group in Montgomery.

The spark that ignited the boycott was an event that symbolized the unjust and humiliating treatment that black citizens had suffered for years. Its elements were Mrs Parks's refusal to relinquish her seat on the segregated bus, the policeman's decision to arrest her, and Rosa Parks's determination to seek justice in a court of law as well as to arouse the defiant spirit of her people.

IKEDA: It was Thursday, 1 December 1955, when Mrs Parks, who had just finished work at a department store, where she was a seamstress, boarded a bus home. She chose to sit near the front of the bus rather than go all the way to the back where the black people were supposed to sit. When the bus driver demanded that she give up her seat to a white man, she refused. Jail time awaited her, but she would not budge or be intimidated.

HARDING: When the policeman arrested Mrs Parks, he asked why she was doing what she was doing. She told the story later: 'I asked him, why did they push us around? And he said, and I quote him, "I don't know, but the law is the law and you are under arrest".'[1] Here, we have a policeman arresting a woman who, in turn, challenged him by appealing to his humanity and sense of fairness.

IKEDA: She posed this fundamental question to awaken the policeman to his own humanity. There is no way to measure the enormity of the suffering and bitter sorrow caused by the injustices of racial discrimination. The humiliating discrimination that black people in Montgomery had lived through for so many years finally provoked a groundswell of indignation. It was the courageous Rosa Parks who opened the floodgates, and out flowed all that pent-up dissatisfaction. Mrs Parks said in retrospect: 'I knew someone had to take the first step. So I made up my mind not to move.'[2]

Dr King described the reason that Rosa Parks did not relinquish her seat on the bus: She had been urged by the zeitgeist – the spirit of the time.

What do you think was the reason that the bus boycott movement became such a powerful force, like a tidal wave across the South?

HARDING: Before I address your question, let me explain something first. I believe that the term *civil rights movement* is an inadequate description for the movement in which we were involved. Oh, there I go – jumping into a debate about terminology.

One of the reasons that I am so adamant about this is that the next generation may be tempted to count up all the civil rights laws and conclude that, 'Oh, now we've got this law and that law, a total of more than seven hundred civil rights laws, so we're finished with this.'

If, instead of referring to the movement as the *civil rights movement*, we spoke in terms of *the expansion of democracy*, then each new generation would recognize that they have a responsibility to expand democracy beyond the way they found it. This duty is an ongoing task that each generation must accept. The question is how to engage the next generation and convey this important message to them. This is a major issue to which, as you can tell, I have passionately devoted myself.

In any case, the bus boycott movement in Montgomery was an important point of departure for the growth of democracy in post-World War II America.

IKEDA: As you say, the human rights movement in which you, Dr King and your colleagues were engaged was not simply an effort to protect the rights of a socially disenfranchised minority. The aim was not to overthrow white rule and supplant it. Rather, it was a movement whose goal was to create a truly democratic society that would wash away the injustice of discrimination and hatred with a tide of justice, thus bringing freedom and humanity.

We can also say that this was a challenge to win peace and

dignity for all humankind. I sincerely hope that the young leaders of tomorrow will learn much from the noble, fearless struggles of the movement's heroes.

HARDING: Another important point to remember is that Dr King did not start the Montgomery bus boycott. When King came to Montgomery, the people were already prepared. The people, primarily members of the Women's Political Council, had already determined that the way black people were treated on the buses was cruel, inhumane and a blow to their dignity. In addition, they knew that the segregation of the buses violated the US Constitution.

Therefore, one of the reasons for the success of the bus boycott movement was that a great deal of discussion and planning had already occurred in the black community. Each participant was already aware of why he or she had joined the boycott.

IKEDA: Everyone was waiting for the moment when they would rise up. Indeed, as you say, the time was ripe for this to happen. In fact, on the same evening that Rosa Parks was arrested, the black leaders of Montgomery, including E. D. Nixon and Ralph Abernathy, sprang into action, and the decision was made to boycott the bus system. Preparations were made in a flash, and the very next day, a Friday, 35,000 fliers were printed and disseminated to every black household to spread the news about the bus boycott (see Conversation Fourteen).

The boycott began on Monday morning, 5 December, four days after Mrs Parks's arrest. Beginning with the first bus leaving the terminal, the usually crowded buses, teeming with black people on their way to work, were almost completely empty. The people had chosen to walk.

Another historic event occurred on this day. The Montgomery Improvement Association was founded to organize the bus boycott, and Dr King accepted the call to be its president.

An Exchange of Energy

Harding: It's important to always recognize that it was the people who called King to lead them. They knew where they wanted to go and what they wanted to do. They told him, in effect: 'You've just received your doctorate in philosophical theology. You are recognized as an educated man in this society. People will listen to you the way that they will not listen to most of us. Be our spokesperson.'

King had to decide how he would respond to this call of the people. According to Coretta, it did not take him long to come to a decision. We all know that becoming a spokesperson for dissenting black people in the Montgomery of 1955 did not simply mean posing for photo ops or composing catchy sound bites for the media. He would be risking his life, and he understood that.

Ikeda: His decision was based on a profound awareness of the implications. The person who recommended Dr King to head the Montgomery Improvement Association was Rufus A. Lewis, the father of one of our Soka Gakkai International members in the United States. As head of the transportation committee, Mr Lewis made a major contribution to the boycott by organizing a carpool system. Dr King praised Lewis's efforts in his first book, the story of the boycott, *Stride Toward Freedom*.

Lewis's daughter was attending college away from home at the time of the boycott and has told us that her parents cautioned her about the dangerous situation in Montgomery. Her parents suggested that she stay at school rather than come home too often. She said, 'They did tell me that if I had to come home for any reason, I should make sure that I didn't ride the buses!'

Harding: So many black parents tried to protect their children from the dangers of such situations. Eventually, the children would take a leading role of their own.

IKEDA: On the evening of 5 December, a mass meeting was called to decide if the boycott, one day old, should be continued. Dr King, as president of the new Montgomery Improvement Association, was to give the keynote speech. The occasion called for a speech that would fire up the people and boost their morale, while at the same time calm them and inhibit a rush to hatred and violence. Could Dr King deliver a message based on these two conflicting objectives? It was a difficult challenge. As Dr King recalled, he entered the highly charged atmosphere of the meeting with a prayer in his heart.[3]

HARDING: In retrospect, it was out of the Montgomery campaign that the mass meeting developed as the main organizing strategy for the freedom movement. People would gather once or twice a week, and sometimes more, to be encouraged, to hear the news, and to vote on and approve actions of the leadership. They would also sing, sing some more and then sing again, building their courage and their hope. These were unifying and joyous occasions, and they were also a factor in the success of the bus boycott movement.

In many of his early speeches, King picked up on themes used by the opposition. Some people in the black community were uncertain about their legal standing and had bought into the assertions of the white establishment. So, in his speech at this first mass meeting, King exposed the false claim by the opposition that boycotting the buses was somehow wrong:

> We are not wrong in what we are doing. If we are wrong, then the Supreme Court of this Nation is wrong. If we are wrong, the Constitution of the United States is wrong. If we are wrong, God Almighty is wrong![4]

King was blessed with such a powerful gift – the capacity to absorb energy from the people. And the energy that he gave back to them boosted their morale and sustained them through the struggle.

IKEDA: This exchange of energy was crucial – Dr King received strength and energy from the people and returned it to them. He gave them unwavering confidence, conviction and hope by establishing the legitimacy and philosophical basis for the bus boycott movement.

He expressed solidarity with the people and generated new energy to propel the movement forward. This is, historically speaking, a formula shared by all successful movements.

HARDING: King told the people that what they were doing was not just for themselves but for the whole country and, indeed, for the whole world. This was the dramatic and powerful context in which King told them that they must see themselves. King had answered the call of the people, and they helped him to define his mission. In turn, he called them to see themselves, awakening them to their own calling. When we think of King the leader, we must never lose sight of this dialectic, this constant sharing between leader and people.

We do a disservice to the whole idea of a people's movement if we attribute the movement's success or failure to the efforts of one charismatic leader. King was inspired by the people, and he inspired them as well. It was a constant give-and-take relationship.

IKEDA: Movements that are firmly rooted in and grow out of the deep experience and consciousness of the people are strong. They are indestructible.

Shortly after the beginning of the boycott, bus companies and Montgomery city officials speculated derisively that as soon as it started raining, black people would start riding the buses again. However, no matter how much it rained, the people continued walking with their heads held high. They did not let themselves be deterred by their opponents' obstructive tactics or threats of violence but stood together and fought back with non-violent courage.

Dr King introduced the following anecdote: An elderly woman who participated in the bus boycott walked day after day. When asked after several weeks of walking whether she was tired, she answered, 'My feets is tired, but my soul is at rest.'[5]

Dr King also described another example:

> Once a carpool driver stopped beside an elderly woman who was trudging along with obvious difficulty. 'Jump in, grandmother,' he said, 'You don't need to walk.' She waved him on. 'I'm not walking for myself,' she explained, 'I'm walking for my children and my grandchildren.'[6]

The success of the Montgomery campaign can be attributed, to a large degree, to the enormous courage and noble sense of mission of ordinary people. The solidarity and commitment of many ordinary people powerfully propelled the bus boycott.

HARDING: This was contrary to what many people had thought at first. The white establishment didn't believe that black people could join together and form a unified organization. Even black people themselves, at one point, doubted their capacity for concerted action. Even so, as the movement gathered strength and solidarity, the people's spirits were buoyed by the encouragement they received from one another.

King directly addressed these themes of solidarity and mission. He said to the people, in effect: 'Look at what you are doing! You are magnificent! You are wonderful!' King never stopped telling them that they were powerful, and their efforts mattered.

I have been trying to emphasize this issue of context – that the power of this movement came from ordinary people who saw their efforts as a contribution to the country and, indeed, to the entire world. And eventually messages of encouragement came from all over the world.

It is undeniable that the success of this movement originated in the determination, courage and endurance of the people. They continued to refuse to use the city bus system for an entire year. Most of the people who depended on the buses were ordinary, working-class people – maids, cooks, janitors and porters. Professionals, by and large, drove their cars wherever they had to go. Ordinary people acted with courage, they saw one another acting courageously, and this was another reason for the success of the boycott.

Also, they realized that everything worthwhile requires sacrifice. They were determined to walk rather than be insulted any longer.

IKEDA: They advanced with pride along the path of justice for the people. In response to the boycott, outrageous harassment and oppressive injustice intensified. False rumours circulated that Dr King was indulging in lavish extravagances. Schemes were hatched to cause internal discord and divisions within the black movement. Dr King was arrested on trivial charges and assaulted daily with many threatening letters and phone calls. But Dr King completely brushed off all threats and assaults on his honour and the movement, continuing to fight bravely alongside the people.

Rejecting Revenge

HARDING: On 30 January 1956, King's home was bombed. I believe that this event hardened King's resolve, and this is what also deepened the people's respect for him. It would become a magnificent opportunity that would test his philosophy of non-violence.

As you probably know, after the bomb blast, people were

outraged, and many rushed to King's house, some bearing weapons, both to protect him and to strike out against whoever had committed this violent act. King then took this wonderful opportunity to remind his supporters that vengeance was not the basis on which their struggle must be carried forth, and he called upon them to lay down their arms and to fight with courage rather than with instruments of brutality. King took every opportunity to call upon the people to rise to a higher level of humanity than that of their oppressors.

IKEDA: Even in the midst of threats on his life, Dr King showed people the spirit of non-violence through his own example. It is true that Dr King was a gifted orator, but we must not overlook the fact that what moved people most were his courageous actions.

Rosa Parks had this to say about Dr King:

> Let us remember that what gave his speeches and sermons legitimacy was that Dr King didn't just talk the talk; he walked the walk from Montgomery to Memphis, enduring jails, beatings, abuse, threats, the bombing of his home, and the highest sacrifice a person can make for a righteous cause.[7]

HARDING: This is another reason for the success of the bus boycott. The people showed that their movement was not based on a desire for revenge or the destruction of the white establishment. They showed that their actions were based on a spiritual philosophy of non-violent resistance to evil, and this is what caught the world's attention and tugged at the conscience of white people, even those right there in Montgomery.

Around that time, the medium of television was beginning to spread to homes across the country, and this was also another reason for the success of the movement. Television focused the attention of supporters from around the country, both black and white, on events in Montgomery, and sympathizers supported the efforts there. For example, people sent shoes to Montgomery for the people who did so much walking during that year, and labour union members donated station wagons for the people to use. These acts of kindness surely helped boost morale and provide encouragement to the people participating in the bus boycott.

IKEDA: One of my favourite quotes by Dr King is 'The universe itself is on the side of freedom and justice.'[8] The struggle for justice, when observed over the long term, has unyielding allies in the forward movement of history and the fundamental principle underlying the universe. Armed with an awareness of this truth, we need to engage in and win our struggle for justice.

The movement next entered a critical stage when Dr King and many activists in the movement were charged with a rarely used 1921 law making conspiracy to interfere with the operation of a business a misdemeanour. Many in the movement, including Dr King, were thrown in jail; no one was afraid or tried to avoid arrest.

Dr King described the situation: 'Those who had previously trembled before the law were now proud to be arrested for the cause of freedom.'[9] In the midst of these trials, the people had been reborn with newfound courage. Dr King also observed: 'There is amazing power in unity. Where there is true unity, every effort to disunite only serves to strengthen the unity.'[10]

Approximately one year after the Montgomery campaign began, the US Supreme Court issued a ruling confirming the unconstitutionality of bus segregation, handing a victory to the bus boycott. The campaign, which began with the refusal by one brave woman, changed hearts and minds, and presented the world with a lesson on the power of non-violence.

This was a movement that brought about a major shift in the society of the time. It was a glorious victory of the spirit – a people's victory and the beginning of a new era in the history of democracy.

HARDING: Through this campaign, the leaders emphasized two main principles. One was that the movement and the way it was conducted were in keeping with the people's own religious beliefs. The second was that the objectives of the movement were entirely consistent with the highest ideals and constitutional legislation of the land. The US Constitution and Christian faith were the two lines of reasoning that King used to support his vision for the movement. The black leaders called upon the country to be true to its Christianity and true to its democratic ideals.

IKEDA: As I have mentioned, the Soka Gakkai was persecuted by Japan's militaristic government during World War II for holding fast to its commitment to justice based on its philosophical convictions. After surviving two years in prison, Josei Toda was released and, looking across the devastated landscape of war-ravaged Japan, exclaimed, 'I want to banish the word *misery* from the face of the Earth.'[11] He rose to the challenge of creating a movement to bring about peace and respect for human rights in Japan, based on Buddhism's philosophy of the sanctity of life.

In those days, the majority of Japanese were in difficult straits, barely surviving. My mentor angrily denounced the coldhearted indifference of the government, which had fallen into disarray and turned a deaf ear to the cries of the people. He questioned the mercilessness and apathy of the government and felt great sympathy for the people. Toda emphasized the importance of ordinary people coming together and raising their voices to speak their wisdom to build a society in which all can realize their full potential.

As Toda's disciple, I took the lead of a people's movement for social change. Consequently, I was unjustly suppressed by the authorities. I was imprisoned for two weeks on trumped-up charges of violating Japan's election laws. This was in 1957, the year after the bus boycott. After a protracted four-and-a-half-year legal battle, my innocence was finally established.[12] My ties to the ordinary heroes who fought by my side and the brave mothers who stood up for justice with me are the most precious treasures of my life.

In the midst of this situation, news of the human rights struggles fought by you, Dr King and your colleagues gave us all tremendous courage. It is an honour and an interesting twist of fate to be carrying on this dialogue with you today.

HARDING: This is surely a testimony to the essential unity that joins us all in the struggle to advance humanity. I trust we can continue to share both our history and our future.

IKEDA: The spirit of fighting for justice based on respect for human dignity transcends time and national boundaries, and resonates with struggles for justice everywhere. Our Soka Gakkai International movement is a struggle of ordinary people who have stood up to make a better world, and we are all immensely proud of this. People discriminated against and oppressed for many years have grown strong and wise and have moved forward, encouraging one another and singing cheerfully, with a firm commitment to transforming society.

As Rabindranath Tagore, one of India's greatest poets and a close friend of Mahatma Gandhi, wrote, 'Man's history is waiting in patience for the triumph of the insulted man.'[13] Those who have suffered the most must be the protagonists creating a new history. Indeed, it is their right.

We can say unreservedly that your movement with Dr King to expand democracy, as well as the people's Soka movement for peace, culture and education, provide powerful testimony for the creation of a new era by ordinary people.

CONVERSATION EIGHT

When Youth Took the Lead

IKEDA: Every major social transformation is born from courageous action. From the success of the Montgomery bus boycott, an enormous sense of courage and confidence radiated outward to those in the civil rights movement. The boycott signalled a point of departure in a long, formidable battle to completely eliminate racial discrimination and to create a more just, democratic American society.

Especially noteworthy is that students and young people played a major role in this historic struggle, burning with a passionate sense of mission. How do you assess the role young people played in the struggle for civil rights?

HARDING: Young people infused the movement with a fresh and powerful energy. Wherever young people joined forces, like in the colleges and other segregated institutions, powerful energy emerged from their recognition of the contradiction between segregation and the democratic ideals preached by the white leaders of the nation that claimed in that Cold War period to be 'leading the free world'. These democratic hopes were ideals taken seriously by many young African Americans. Indeed, young people were a force for change that helped spread the movement and challenge the nation to live up to its best possibilities.

The Montgomery bus boycott was successfully concluded by the winter of 1956. Following that, in May 1957, a youth-oriented Prayer Pilgrimage for Freedom was held in Washington, DC, but during that time, there was no sustained or widespread freedom movement activity. Then, in the early 1960s, the youth burst into the limelight with the power and dynamism to open up a new front in the movement.

IKEDA: My mentor proclaimed that it is the passion and power of youth that will create the new century. Indeed, nothing is more powerful than the energy of youth, burning with a passion for justice.

In those days, Dr King was head of the Southern Christian Leadership Conference and travelled tirelessly all over the South and the nation, sharing news of the movement. In 1957 and 1958, Dr King delivered more than two hundred speeches. At each location, Dr King would sow the seeds of freedom, hope and courage. Partly in response to his impassioned call, the youth rose up to initiate a new campaign that was uniquely their own.

HARDING: The youth took the lead, and in the spring of 1960 students all over the South began the sit-in movement. Young people were not waiting for King to act, rather they were inspired and strengthened by his message to implement the actions that they felt they needed to carry out. They did not sit around waiting for him to lead them. It is important to understand that the youth movement was not dependent on King. It derived its inspiration from him and took off in its own directions.

Also, it is important to know that there were a number of young white people among the students who rose up to participate in the movement. Some of these young people had grown up in the stifling world of the white South, and they had to make hard and costly decisions to join their black comrades in the work to create a world that their parents could not imagine.

IKEDA: This is an important aspect of this history. One of these white youths was Harvey Cox, now a world-renowned professor emeritus of religious studies at Harvard University. Dr Cox was about the same age as Dr King, and I understand that the two first met when Dr Cox was studying one summer at Vanderbilt University in Nashville, Tennessee (1956). At the time, Dr Cox was contemplating doing work related to the elimination of racial discrimination, and he was impressed by Dr King, who had come to the university to give a talk. Eventually, the two met, and Dr King invited Dr Cox to speak at various conferences and participate in marches with him.

Dr Cox has emphasized that he was drawn to Dr King's genuine courage and unwavering commitment to the philosophy of non-violence. I am sure that many people felt the same way. The enormous, irresistible appeal of Dr King's speeches was found in the way he inspired profound courage in people and gave them firm conviction in the movement, encouraging them to combine words with action, just as he did.

HARDING: King's most important role was travelling the entire United States and explaining to people what was happening in the movement and the significance of these events. He had a superb capacity that he brought to that task. The majority of people in African-American society had close historic relationships with the Christian church and were accustomed to the language and teachings of the church, so they recognized in King's message a familiar voice. He spoke in a language that they understood. Even if they could not grasp every element, they were certain that it was right.

They also knew that King was not just a great orator; this was someone speaking out of the demanding experience of his courageous life. They knew that his message was grounded in the religious faith that had kept them going through generations of difficult trials.

IKEDA: This is a point that leaders should heed. The people are wise. Young people can easily see right through hypocrisy and deception. Dr King's words of conviction, backed by courageous action, sparked an ardent passion in the hearts of many youth.

HARDING: A striking example of the rise of youth in the black freedom movement is the group that began the sit-ins at lunch counters in North Carolina in 1960. Much later, I spoke with several of the original participants. I asked what had inspired and encouraged them to begin the sit-ins that would eventually spread throughout the South and even to some parts of the northern United States.

The young men mentioned that their inspiration had come primarily from two sources. One was Dr King. By the time they took action in February 1960, King had already been travelling around the South, telling people about the Montgomery campaign and encouraging them to work for necessary social changes in their communities. They had heard King and been inspired by him when he visited their communities.

Their second source of inspiration was their extraordinary high school and college teachers. Many of them had been encouraged by these teachers.

IKEDA: I believe the first sit-in was held by four students from North Carolina College of Agriculture and Technical Arts. To protest the policy of racial segregation, the students sat down at a whites-only lunch counter, determined to sit there until they were served and, in effect, recognized as human beings and equal citizens. The students sat in silent dignity at the lunch counter while bystanders tormented them with obnoxious pranks such as dumping catsup and mayonnaise on their heads and down the backs of their shirts. The students stoically endured this harassment and continued their non-violent resistance, even when the police arrested them and put them in jail.

Dr King praised the brave students who participated in the sit-ins and celebrated the significance of their actions. He said that when these young men sat down at that lunch counter, they were actually standing up for what is best in the promise of the American dream – a dream that was meant for every person in the country. The dedicated, fearless actions of these youth aroused in other youth the same passion for justice and a desire to join the battle. The surge of this energy spread rapidly throughout the South.

New Ways of Living

HARDING: Martin was always open to young people and urged them to recognize that they had a crucial role to play in the transformation of their nation. Eventually, as often happens with young people, the youths whom he encouraged began to have their own ideas, and they ventured out on a more independent path. So, like a good parent, he had to be willing to let them explore their own mission because he had encouraged them to do their own work.

For instance, King never participated in the Freedom Rides, which were the next major stage of the movement, but the youth were fully involved. Many of them were badly beaten during the Freedom Rides, an action that eventually eliminated the segregation laws and practices in interstate travel all over the nation.

IKEDA: The Freedom Rides were a movement in which black and white people would take long-distance bus trips to test whether bus terminals and other travel facilities were desegregated in compliance with recent court rulings. These people were frequently harassed and brutally assaulted by white citizens; some were beaten unconscious and seriously injured. Nevertheless, they heroically maintained their non-violent stance. Dr King at every opportunity praised the young people's unwavering courage and commitment to non-violence and asserted that historians of the future would surely look back upon the Freedom Rides as one of the most precious legacies of the country.[1]

HARDING: Martin highly praised the courage of the youth. Of course, he wasn't always sure that they used wisdom in all their decisions, but that's why young people and older people need to work together. King saw young people as part of the foundation of the 'beloved community', the ideal community that he envisioned. He felt this way because he believed that young people had not experienced as much disappointment and discouragement in their lives and did not harbour as much fear or prejudice as older people. Because of this and their courage and creativity, he believed that young people brought a new spirit to the movement. He saw their wonderful possibilities, and besides he was only thirty-one himself when the sit-in movement began – still a young man.

We discussed earlier Ella Baker's contributions to this young people's movement (see Conversation Five). As you recall, it was she who encouraged young people from various southern locations to come together in April 1960 to form an organization. Eventually, the young people who had spread the movement through their sit-ins and other desegregation actions all over the South formed the organization I mentioned earlier called the Student Nonviolent Coordinating Committee.

IKEDA: In October 1960, the year when the sit-in movement was spreading in the South, I happened to be visiting the United States.

I was on my first tour of cities in the United States and Canada – first of all, Honolulu, then San Francisco, Seattle, Chicago, Toronto, New York, Washington, DC and Los Angeles – to visit with and encourage Soka Gakkai members in these areas.

In those days, our international members were few and in the United States mainly consisted of Japanese Americans and Japanese women who had come to the United States as war brides. I listened to their concerns and did my best to provide encouragement to the women, many of whom could not speak English well and, knowing almost no one, had endured many difficulties alone in unfamiliar circumstances. I advised them to master English and learn to drive in order to become active in American society. In time, these pioneers became trusted community members who could support and aid others in need.

In New York, I went to the United Nations Headquarters and observed the General Assembly. That year, many youthful African leaders of newly independent countries participated. Seeing them gave me the impression that the twenty-first century was going to be the Century of Africa, and I mentioned this to the young people in our group. I understand that the independence struggles of many of these African nations had no small effect on young African Americans of the period.

Dr King wrote, 'Frequently, I heard [my people] say that if their African brothers could break the bonds of colonialism, surely the American Negro could break Jim Crow.'[2] Encouraged by the independence of these African countries, Dr King and the youth stood up fearlessly and with perseverance to meet the challenge of bringing democratic change to their communities and the country.

Harding: Young people are drawn to the call to work for change – then as well as now. They are receptive to the idea of creating new futures. These days, young Americans have been told that they should seek security and a safe existence more than anything else.

However, in the early 1960s, young people felt that they had to abandon security and take risks in order to create new possibilities for themselves, their country and their local communities.

Young people are indeed attracted to this kind of calling. Something inside them makes them want to try new things, including new ways of living and acting. Our tendency as adults is to try to keep them on the path that we believe is 'safe', but if we want to nurture growth and development in young people, we have to realize that they may not always do what we think they should do. If we want to encourage them to follow their deepest convictions, wherever those may lead – as long as they are seeking increased human development – then we have to give them time and space to explore new paths. It may seem that these new directions are risky, but they are necessary to achieve social change.

IKEDA: This is something that we must take to heart. One aspect of Dr King's greatness is that he awakened young people to their true mission, giving them pride in the nobility of an honourable life and in the value of contributing to other people's lives and to society. Those whose hearts are filled with hope and ideals, and who maintain the strength of their convictions are strong. These are also the happiest people.

Mrs King shared that her husband often told the children that if you don't take risks in life for something you believe in strongly, there's no meaning in life. He also said that it's not how *long* you live that is important, it's *how* you live your life.

HARDING: King's leadership was supported in many important ways by his wife's understanding of his role as a change agent in the movement for democratic transformation in this country. Coretta had, even before meeting King, received an intense anti-war education. She attended Antioch College in Ohio, a progressive institution of higher learning, where she was influenced by philosophies espousing anti-war, anti-capitalism and other social change concepts.

I believe that it was because Coretta was exposed to all these ideas before she met King that she could be a strong partner for him. Besides encouraging and supporting him, she understood exactly what was happening and what was at stake.

A great advantage for King was that he could talk to Coretta about important issues facing him and the movement. She was a true comrade for him, and she would never hold him back from carrying out the mission that was his to pursue. Besides that, she herself was a rich source of ideas and inspiration.

IKEDA: Dr King wrote with utmost appreciation, 'If I have done anything in this struggle, it is because I have had behind me and at my side a devoted, understanding, dedicated, patient companion in the person of my wife.'[3]

As Nichiren wrote, 'It is the power of the bow that determines the flight of the arrow . . . and the strength of the wife that guides the actions of her husband.'[4] This is true in every era.

It is impossible to imagine the weight of the heavy responsibility and pressures placed on King's shoulders during a period of complex, turbulent social change. In this sense, Coretta's presence by his side, sharing that heavy load and supporting him, must have been an immeasurable blessing.

HARDING: The Southern Christian Leadership Conference was composed of black Protestant ministers who were activists like King. As the name indicates, it was made up of people who considered themselves leaders. When King took on this heavy responsibility, please remember, it was 1957 and King was just twenty-eight. He was still a young man in the process of maturing.

To add to that, he had to deal with many individuals in the organization who had large egos. King had to learn how to deal with many people who held strong opinions about what needed to be done to heal the soul of America. This was a difficult task.

President Ikeda, you were just thirty-two when you became president of the Soka Gakkai, weren't you?

Songs of Liberation and Solidarity

IKEDA: Yes. At that time, there were many leaders senior to me in the organization, but there was a consensus on the board of directors to ask me to accept the office of president, because I was the direct disciple of Josei Toda. However, I thought I was too young.

I was also still under a cloud of suspicion, having been accused, albeit falsely, of violating national election laws, and the case was still in court. It was not until January 1962 that I was finally acquitted. Frankly, I wanted to wait until the court case was over, and we had won. However, I could not continue refusing their insistent requests. After observing the second anniversary of my beloved mentor's passing, I was inaugurated as third president on 3 May 1960.

After the ceremony, I returned home, and nothing seemed out of the ordinary. My wife had prepared a typically plain and frugal evening meal. In Japan, it is customary to celebrate with *osekihan*, a traditional rice dish cooked with adzuki beans. When I saw that we were having our usual fare, I commented, 'I thought we might be having *osekihan* to celebrate the occasion, but . . .'

My wife came right out and said that she no longer considered our home to have a husband. She had not prepared *osekihan* because, she said, 'I consider your inauguration ceremony a funeral service.'[5]

After that, as 3 May approached every year, my wife told me that she would think to herself, 'Ah, he's still alive.' She had in the back of her mind that my mentor had died seven years after his inauguration as Soka Gakkai president. On the eighth anniversary of my inauguration, my wife finally prepared *osekihan* to celebrate the occasion. My wife and I were determined to gladly sacrifice ourselves for the happiness of our dear Soka Gakkai friends and the cause of building a peaceful society.

Returning to our discussion, do you have any recollections of Dr King's family life that you can share?

HARDING: I know that King felt guilty and sad about not spending as much time as he would have liked with his children. I don't know what kinds of discussions he had with his wife, but I do know that Coretta always wanted to support her husband to the fullest extent she could. She was a woman who always spoke her mind. Also, she had a wonderful sense of humour, which often came in handy.

In King's case, it was inevitable that the path he chose would have major trade-offs and influences on his life. I believe that he did his utmost to be the best father that he could be.

I must say that I'm sure if you and Mrs Ikeda had met Dr King and Coretta Scott King, you would have had an interesting discussion.

IKEDA: Somehow, I feel that through our dialogue I am conversing with Dr King, for which I am grateful. Also, I am glad to know that many young Japanese people have been reading and thoroughly enjoying our serialized dialogue.

HARDING: I'm glad that they are interested. One more important aspect of youth participation in the movement was their joy of singing. They attended all the meetings and assemblies and were in every instance the primary song leaders. They channelled such magnificent energy and spirit into their singing. The freedom songs that they led us in singing were mostly based on songs from the church that were transformed in the course of the movement.

This is one example that eloquently reveals the youthful creativity that was so important. As the singing was going on in the mass meetings, the youth took the original songs and made them more modern by changing the words slightly and using a different rhythm and beat.

There is no doubt that singing was an important facet of the movement. In so many instances, we know that people sang when they were in grave danger or in jail.

One of the best-known songs of the movement was 'We Shall Overcome'. This was originally an African-American church song called 'I'll Overcome Someday'. It was used in the labour movement when black people began to work with white labour activists in the 1930s and 1940s, and brought their songs with them.

The singer and labour activist Pete Seeger changed the words and title to 'We Shall Overcome' sometime in the late 1940s. Then, as labour movement activists began to work even more closely with the freedom movement, the song developed further, with the addition of new verses.

IKEDA: 'We Shall Overcome' became well-known in Japan and was sung widely at youth gatherings and in student movement activities. A song can touch people's hearts and rouse them to action. Song creates a powerful sense of spiritual liberation and solidarity.

Dr King spoke about and believed in the power of song. In the summer of 1962 in Albany, Georgia, Dr King was thrown into jail. Other participants of a demonstration there had also been arrested and were admitted to the jail one after another. As new people came in, they would proudly sing freedom songs at the top of their voices. Dr King wrote later that he could hear them from his cell, their voices giving him courage and comfort.

It was the same in the Soka Gakkai's history. When we were oppressed by unjust powers, we raised our voices in song as we withstood their assaults. Songs were born in the midst of our struggles for peace and human rights, and we surged forward courageously with these songs in our hearts. The forward momentum of the Soka Gakkai has always been in concert with the voices of the people, singing for justice.

HARDING: I often think that one crucial aspect of the freedom songs was the courage they gave to people. Sometimes, people would be in dangerous situations and would sing: 'We are not afraid. We are not afraid.'

To be clear, they were not singing about how unafraid they were. In fact, they were often trembling with fear. What they were singing about was their determination to not let fear overcome them. They meant: 'We are not going to let fear conquer us. We are not going to let fear stop us.' The encouragement they gave one another through singing was an important element in the life of the movement and its participants.

Sometimes, the songs included great humour. One of the songs that people loved to sing had these words: 'If you come to the back of the bus, and you can't find me anywhere, just come on up to the front of the bus, and I'll be riding up there.' And songs evolved over time also – by the mid-1960s, people were singing, 'If you come to the back of the bus, and you can't find me anywhere, just come on up to the front of the bus, and I'll be *driving* up there.'

Songs were so important to the movement. Without songs, many people would not have been able to bear the many hardships they had to face in the struggle.

One day, my brother, I hope that you will have a chance to meet one of the song leaders and teachers of the freedom movement, a woman named Bernice Johnson Reagon, who grew up in Albany, Georgia. She would not only be happy to teach you the songs, she would tell you their stories much more fully than I can. She is my friend and former student, and I am grateful for her wisdom and gifts.

Ikeda: I would love to meet Dr Reagon someday.

Songs that emerge from the people's lives and experiences will be handed down and sung for generations to come. My mentor often said that wherever one finds a flourishing group of people, one will also find music and song.

In this spirit, aiming to send courage and hope to as many of my friends as possible, and in the hope that they will move forward courageously and cheerfully, I have written or helped write many songs, and we have sung them walking arm in arm.

The creation of a new history is always accompanied by strong, robust musical expression. In the Soka Gakkai International, this is our belief and conviction.

CONVERSATION NINE

The Pivotal Struggle in Birmingham

IKEDA: This famous poem is by Langston Hughes, whom you mentioned earlier as a favourite of yours (see Conversation Two):

Being walkers with the dawn and morning,
Walkers with the sun and morning,
We are not afraid of night,
Nor days of gloom,
Nor darkness,
Being walkers with the sun and morning.[1]

It was the fearless advancement of the youth and the courageous actions of the people that brought a new dawn of success in the civil rights movement. As we have recounted in previous conversations, the brave actions of ordinary people, such as those who took part in the bus boycott and sit-ins, broke through the thick walls of adversity.

Through the pivotal struggle in Birmingham, the momentum of these ordinary people ultimately spread the movement throughout the nation and drew the world's attention. The Birmingham campaign played a significant role in the subsequent development of the movement.

HARDING: The Birmingham campaign took place in the spring of 1963, the year marking the hundredth anniversary of President Lincoln's announcement of the Emancipation Proclamation, which opened the way for the official end of the institution of slavery in America. In the period leading up to the spring of 1963, many movement organizations adopted the hopeful slogan 'Free by '63', expressing the determination of black people to achieve freedom and equality within the century of the Emancipation Proclamation.

However, even after the victorious Montgomery bus boycott, cruel and inhumane racial discrimination, including the segregation of public accommodations, remained the practice in many southern states as well as many states in the North.

Despite the 1955 Brown II ruling of the US Supreme Court,[2] which addressed the implementation of racial desegregation in public education, the reality in the South changed hardly at all. In fact, by 1963, there were troubling signs that segregation was worsening.

At that point, many thought that if a victory could be won in a city like Birmingham – which was considered the most racially segregated and terrorized city in the entire country – it would be a major breakthrough and would stimulate significant progress in the freedom movement. Around that time, the Reverend Fred Shuttlesworth and other local pastors central in advancing the freedom movement invited King to Birmingham, and preparations began for a new campaign. It was early in the spring of 1963 when the Birmingham campaign began in earnest.

IKEDA: In January of that year, I again visited Hawaii, Los Angeles and New York after an absence of more than two years. Our Soka

Gakkai peace and human rights movement was still in its infancy in the United States. In April 1963, when I heard the news that the Birmingham campaign had begun, I had a keen sense that a new era was being born.

Dr King and his colleagues were resolute in their commitment to the movement. In *Why We Can't Wait*, Dr King wrote:

> Along with Fred Shuttlesworth, we believed that while a campaign in Birmingham would surely be the toughest fight of our civil-rights careers, it could, if successful, break the back of segregation all over the nation.[3]

Leap courageously into the worst situations! Achieve a stunning breakthrough! Overcome that first obstacle, and the opportunity for progress in other places will be vastly improved! Seen from a historical viewpoint, this is an important formula for success in any struggle for change. This strategic approach was also that of my mentor, who trained me by continually putting me in charge of the most difficult tasks.

To build the foundation for the Birmingham campaign, Dr King, first of all, sought to unify the black community by speaking to numerous small groups in town after town, thoroughly discussing the objectives and principles of the struggle. Dr King urged the people to stand up courageously in a non-violent struggle to win their freedom and equality. He stressed the imperative of breaking down the formal and informal structures of white supremacy.

At every meeting, Dr King spoke of the power of non-violence. He wrote: 'We proved . . . that we needed no [physical] weapons – not so much as a toothpick. We proved that we possessed the most formidable weapon of all – the conviction that we were right.'[4]

HARDING: In every movement, the people's sincere acceptance and understanding are essential. To achieve this understanding, it is crucial to develop open, one-on-one conversations wherever possible, which means that small gatherings play a major role. No matter how small the group, when people get to know and understand one another and share their thoughts and opinions, they can discover a path to new possibilities and unexpected transformation. This is a point that I discussed with students at Soka University of America.

In the 1960s, King continued with these quiet and sincere dialogues, speaking to groups small and large in every part of the South. King was the best-known, but not the only, spokesperson for the movement and was also responsible – along with other leaders – for a variety of efforts designed to expand and develop the movement, first in the South, then later in the North, when it spread there.

He reflected long and hard, trying to identify the most effective methods of non-violent struggle and to discern, together with the cooperation of his colleagues, the next steps to advance the movement. King also played a critical role in the fundraising activities that helped to make the movement's organizing activities possible.

IKEDA: Financial resources are a critical reality and a valuable lifeline in every movement. Toda took upon himself the serious task of supporting our organization's finances in its early days – despite the challenging political and economic situation created by Japan's rapid shift to militarism – in order to realize Makiguchi's vision.

I understand that, especially in the Birmingham campaign, there were major financial difficulties. After Dr King succeeded in unifying the black community, he became all the more determined to participate in the marches and was prepared to be arrested and thrown into jail. However, when four or five hundred people had been arrested, there was not enough money to post bail and release them from jail.

As a result, some people started saying that Dr King should refrain from participating in the demonstrations because when he was in jail, he was unable to continue fundraising. This meant that the people in jail would likely have to stay there. Dr King had to make an agonizingly difficult decision. If he continued the campaign as planned and failed to raise funds, all the people who believed in him and in the leadership, and had summoned their courage to participate in the marches and face arrest and possible imprisonment, might, as a result, be abandoned in jail. But ultimately, he decided that the only way to vanquish the injustice and discrimination that inflicted suffering on tens of millions of people was to continue moving forward for the greater cause, no matter the obstacles.

Dr King participated in the marches with this determination and an acceptance of whatever lay ahead. As a result, he was arrested and sent to jail.

HARDING: No one knows how much a leader of such a danger-fraught movement for democracy has to wrestle with and agonize over each and every decision.

IKEDA: I sympathize completely.

Regarding the bail bonds, one of our SGI-USA members, a child during the civil rights movement, proudly shared with her fellow members her cherished memories of her participation. She recalled that Dr King had been arrested and jailed somewhere and to post bail for him and other boycott participants, her mother cooked food to sell to raise money. She nostalgically remembered helping her mother with the food sales.

I am sure that Dr King's spirits were buoyed by the heartfelt support of each of these earnest, industrious people and that he drew from them the courage he needed to move forward.

HARDING: He always felt energized by the people and was grateful for their support. His courage and the courage of the wonderfully ordinary people of Birmingham's black community inspired black public figures in the North, like the entertainers Harry Belafonte and Sidney Poitier, to take extraordinary steps to help raise money for the cause, especially the necessary bail-bond money.

Because of his loyalty to the many ordinary people who made up the movement, it is not surprising that King chose to participate in the marches in Birmingham. During the march on 12 April 1963, he and other marchers were arrested and jailed. The letter he wrote from jail during this time is a precious historical document that reveals his thoughts and convictions. I was present when one of Martin's lawyers brought it out of the prison.

Injustice Anywhere is a Threat to Justice Everywhere

IKEDA: This was the famous 'Letter from Birmingham Jail', wasn't it?[5] Dr King wrote this letter in response to a statement by a group of local white pastors. Their letter, criticizing the protest activities of Dr King and his colleagues, was published in the Birmingham newspaper.[6] Dr King had read their statement while incarcerated and immediately authored a long rebuttal. He wrote on the available white space and margins of newspapers as well as on sheets of writing paper secretly sent in by his staff, lawyers and fellow activists.

HARDING: Eight white pastors had signed the public statement critical of King and the movement's activities. Some of the pastors were prominent in the local white community. In their statement, they called for a halt to the anti-segregation protests, describing them as 'unwise and untimely'.[7]

In his response, King addressed the leaders of the white churches directly. He appealed to their consciences and questioned their prior silence and their lack of Christian leadership in the face of the evils of racial discrimination and segregation.

IKEDA: The pastors maintained that the protests 'incite hatred and violence, however technically peaceful those actions may be'.[8] Dr King countered, clarifying why it was necessary to take action and to do so now. He asked the pastors why they criticized those who raised their voices to protest the suffering they endured while remaining silent about the fundamental evil of racial segregation. King suggested that this was akin to 'condemning the robbed man because his possession of money precipitated the evil act of robbery'.[9]

HARDING: King saw that instead of condemning the evil itself, the white pastors were condemning the people trying to remove the evil because, according to the pastors, their actions seemed to precipitate violence. There was no condemnation of the people creating the evil and no condemnation of the people violently retaliating against the non-violent protesters. And certainly no condemnation of the silent white majority.

In his letter, King especially tried to express his deep disappointment with the white Christian churches. He said he had hoped that the leaders of those churches would courageously stand together with their black brothers and sisters on the common ground of their faith in the loving Jesus.

King could have reminded them that Jesus teaches us that wherever we are working for the weak and the poor and the outcasts, we are working for him. Instead, King spoke of the great temptation of religious leaders to identify not with the exploited outcasts of society but with the powerful leaders of the status quo. Indeed, he pointed out that they not only identified with the status quo, they went to great lengths to justify it and condemn those trying to change it.

IKEDA: The white pastors also criticized Dr King and his supporters as 'outsiders' coming into Birmingham to agitate and stir up trouble. Dr King argued pointedly: 'I am in Birmingham because injustice is here . . . Injustice anywhere is a threat to justice everywhere. We are caught in an inescapable network of mutuality, tied in a single garment of destiny.'[10]

Injustice is evil no matter where it occurs. We must not be apathetic and uncaring in the face of injustice when we think it does not directly affect us. We must take Dr King's statement seriously and engrave it in our hearts.

We cannot say that we live in a just world if injustice runs rampant anywhere in it. We must stand up strongly for those who suffer the ravages of injustice. Dr King described this as the ability to understand and willingly share the suffering of others.

In Buddhism, we call this the 'spirit of empathy' and believe that carrying this spirit in our hearts and engaging in altruistic actions on behalf of others are the marks of true faith. The reason that the Soka Gakkai International has developed a grassroots citizens' movement in 192 countries and territories is that we have been unflaggingly committed to working together with people to alleviate their hardships and misfortunes.

In his 'Letter from Birmingham Jail', Dr King made a frank, forceful appeal to people of faith to find it within their hearts to support and work for justice.

HARDING: Throughout his letter, King was telling these religious leaders that they needed to allow themselves to empathize with the oppressed and to refrain from distancing themselves from them. King appealed to their humanity.

For example, he asked them to think about how they would explain to their child why he or she could not go to an amusement park that had been advertised on television. How would they explain to their child that it was closed to 'coloured' people? He wanted these so-called religious leaders to imagine what that meant.

King wanted people to think in terms of all humanity, not simply in terms of black or white labels. And he especially wanted members of the white churches to realize that they were hiding behind their whiteness, shielding themselves from acknowledging the humanity and the pain of black people, keeping themselves from empathizing with blacks' suffering – just because they were black. He essentially told the leadership of the white churches that they could have helped to guide their members to a more enlightened and supportive view of the black struggle. He also demonstrated, by example, that he loved these white pastors, in spite of what they had written in their statement.

At this moment, King understood his responsibility to be the one to remind these leaders of their own highest calling. He urged them to challenge themselves. He asked them how they could, as persons identifying themselves as ministers of the Christ, follow the way of Jesus in their hometown.

His focus was not so much to condemn them but to ask them: 'Do you see what your role is supposed to be? Do you understand that you are missing an opportunity to fulfil your responsibilities here?'

IKEDA: Dr King's letter was a well-reasoned, convincing statement overflowing with power and passion. His warmly expressed trust in humanity undoubtedly impressed readers profoundly. Dr King ended his letter with this appeal:

> Let us all hope that the dark clouds of racial prejudice will soon pass away and the deep fog of misunderstanding will be lifted from our fear-drenched communities, and in some not too distant tomorrow the radiant stars of love and brotherhood will shine over our great nation with all their scintillating beauty.[11]

HARDING: King expressed such hope, despite the fact that he was writing from a jail cell. He never lost his love for, and faith in, humanity. Freed after spending about a week in jail, he then returned to lead the non-violent campaign in Birmingham.

During the next stage of the struggle, the Birmingham movement found a new source of energy. It was in the enthusiastic, courageous participation of high school, middle school and elementary school students.

THE FEARLESSNESS OF YOUTH

IKEDA: This was a dramatic development indeed. Throughout his life, Dr King placed his hope in young people. Concerning the participation of youth in Birmingham, he wrote, 'We believed they would have the courage to respond to our call.'[12]

However, it seemed that Dr King also felt some understandable hesitation in asking children and young people to be involved in the movement, given the serious dangers. I can understand his concern completely.

HARDING: Once again, young people inspired their elders and took risks that we thought older people would not take. The youth stood bravely in the face of police attack dogs, sometimes dancing to express their determination before being roughly knocked down by the fire hoses. To return to your quote from Langston Hughes, they were 'walkers with the sun and morning / not afraid of the night'. They were much freer from the chains of social and economic responsibility that often bind people to the status quo. The participation of young people breathed a fresh, vibrant, sun-like energy into the heart of the people's movement, bringing a bold and fearless sense of adventure – an attitude that most older people lacked.

At the same time, however, there was the traditional social

protocol in the South, especially in black society, which the young people observed; they respected their elders. This was an interesting dialectic: The young people leapt into action on the frontlines, moving toward leadership in many ways, yet they also recognized that the elders were still the elders and were due their respect and appreciation.

The young people understood the importance of their role in society more clearly and accurately than adults gave them credit for. They marched courageously, singing freedom songs and maintaining their commitment to non-violent action, holding their heads high as they were attacked, arrested and jailed.

On the first day of the Birmingham youth march, the authorities showed restraint, but on the following day, 3 May, they turned fire hoses on the marchers, including the young people and children. The blasts of water struck the young people and children so forcefully that they were swept off their feet, slammed into walls and onto the roadway and their clothes were torn and ripped from their bodies.

In other situations, they faced the threat of police dogs. But the young people refused to give up.

IKEDA: Another SGI-USA member recalls that she happened to be in the area where the violence against the marchers occurred. She and her two young children were shocked by the horrific scene of police brutality that unfolded before them. She said that she simultaneously felt deep sadness and terror.

This kind of behaviour should never have happened and should never be tolerated. This much should be clear.

HARDING: I agree completely. I am eternally grateful for the young people who insisted on maintaining the best of their humanity. On 5 May, youth and adults gathered again to continue marching. Just as before, the order to turn the fire hoses on the marchers was given. However, this time, the firemen of the Birmingham Fire Department refused to obey the order, and the water was not discharged. Undoubtedly, their consciences would not permit them to inflict even more violence on the non-violent marchers.

The force of public opinion also played a decisive role in the campaign. The images of police ordering their attack dogs upon the non-violent marchers and turning powerful hoses upon children had been broadcast throughout the world, and the response was a thunderous public outcry of criticism and condemnation. The Kennedy administration knew this was a severe blow to their self-appointed Cold War role as 'leaders of the free world'. Immediately, the White House and US Department of Justice sent their representatives to participate in (and speed up) the negotiations that were taking place between the leaders of the movement and some of the local white community leaders.

IKEDA: One could say that Dr King and his campaign of non-violence was a struggle to awaken and enlighten the hearts and minds of those discriminating against black people and to lead them toward self-transformation.

HARDING: King maintained the belief that the idea and practice of white supremacy was harmful to black people as well as everyone else – including white people, especially white children. Therefore, King thought that we must devote ourselves to loving white people and to working to create a 'more perfect Union', and that this required overcoming white supremacy.

Partly through the efforts of white allies doing anti-racism work in the white community, we are now discovering how the teaching of white supremacy gives white people a completely false sense of reality and damages them deeply, beginning in childhood.

King was always expanding and moving forward with his work, not just for the sake of black people but to heal society. What would a healed America be like? This would make a wonderful subject for contemplating the shape of our future and for developing curriculum at Soka University of America. Of course, laws are important, but building a healed society involves much more than enacting a law.

IKEDA: The root of the English word *heal* originally included the meanings 'totality' and 'completeness', and the word *health* has the same root. In this sense, a healed society would be a society that has discovered its sense of wholeness and has achieved equality for every person. This would be a society in which the social system and its laws serve the people. It would be a society in which people respect one another and live with dignity and equality. They would share a deep trust in one another, come to one another's aid, and grow and learn from one another. These are some of the most important objectives of our Soka Gakkai International movement.

The Birmingham campaign propelled the freedom movement forward with new energy as it garnered a massive outpouring of support from all around the country and influenced public opinion. At the same time, it powerfully inspired others working for freedom and democracy across the globe.

On 10 May, Reverend Shuttlesworth and Dr King announced to reporters that an agreement had been reached with city officials. This would begin to desegregate lunch counters, restrooms, drinking fountains, and fitting rooms, allow for hiring black workers in stores as salesclerks, and also release all the jailed demonstrators.

HARDING: It was an important victory, but the violence did not stop. That next evening, the hotel in which King had been staying and his brother's house were bombed. Angry black community members, untrained in non-violence, sought to retaliate. This moved President Kennedy to dispatch federal troops to bring the situation under control. Then on 20 May, the US Supreme Court ruled that Birmingham's Jim Crow laws violated the Constitution.

IKEDA: On 11 June, responding to the situation in Birmingham and the dozens of other cities where action had been inspired by Birmingham, President Kennedy spoke to the nation, introducing a civil rights bill and asking for legislation that would ban discrimination in public accommodations and protect the right to vote for all Americans.

Kennedy appealed to the American people and pointed to the fundamental moral question facing them:

> One hundred years of delay have passed since President Lincoln freed the slaves . . . Now the time has come for this Nation to fulfill its promise. The events in Birmingham and elsewhere have so increased the cries for equality that no city or State or legislative body can prudently choose to ignore them . . . I shall ask the Congress of the United States to act, to make a commitment it has not fully made in this century to the proposition that race has no place in American life or law.[13]

The times were changing. The walls that had seemed so indestructible before were now crumbling.

During this period, I had been preparing for a planned meeting with President Kennedy. But later that year, he was assassinated, and I regret that I never got to meet this great man.

The victory in Birmingham unleashed a tidal wave of energy in the movement for freedom and justice, and this led to the next historic moment, which was the March on Washington.

CONVERSATION TEN

The March on Washington

IKEDA: History is made in the present. Struggling day after day in the real world and winning one small victory after another, each generation inherits and seeks to realize the noble dreams of preceding generations. There is no greater adventure than participating in this mission.

As Dr King aptly declared, 'In the summer of 1963, the Negroes of America wrote an emancipation proclamation to themselves.'[1] His statement indicated that, in the year marking the hundredth anniversary of Abraham Lincoln's Emancipation Proclamation, the civil rights movement, which had triumphed in the Birmingham campaign, surged forward to a new stage in its development. The event that symbolized this great progress was the March on Washington for Jobs and Freedom, held on Wednesday, 28 August 1963 – a day that changed history.

At that time, I had been Soka Gakkai president just three years. In the midst of my hectic schedule, traversing the entire Japanese archipelago, I was intently focused on the progress of the civil rights movement.

How precisely did this historic gathering come about?

HARDING: I was involved in some of the early conversations in Birmingham that eventually led to the March on Washington. The powerful Birmingham campaign had ended by midyear, and we needed to respond to the widespread yearning of the people for more action toward freedom.

In keeping with our tendency as Americans, many people in the movement had the sense that things were moving too slowly, that we needed to develop a more robust strategy to impress on the country the great urgency and need for social change. As you probably know, my friend, in the Birmingham period there were hundreds of other freedom movement campaigns in other communities attacking segregation and many related forms of racial injustice. In addition, the Birmingham campaign had pushed President Kennedy, his brother, Attorney General Robert Kennedy, and many of their official and unofficial group of advisors to see the need for federal commitment to civil rights as represented by presidentially initiated congressional action.

For King and other movement leaders, the original idea was for a massive march on Washington with participants literally streaming into the capital from every part of the country, demanding the passage of strong civil rights legislation.

So, this was the context for the beginning of the conversations about the March on Washington, a major event that indeed drew people from every region of the country.

IKEDA: I imagine that people felt the time had come for more change – for a new era to begin. Or perhaps we could say that they themselves created the new era.

According to US Department of Justice statistics, in the span of two-and-a-half months after the Birmingham campaign, a total of 758 demonstrations were held in 186 cities across the country.

During this period, an average of ten protests were held every day somewhere in the United States.

Dr King wrote about the far-reaching impact of the movement:

> Freedom was contagious. Its fever boiled in nearly one thousand cities, and by the time it had passed its peak, many thousands of lunch counters, hotels, parks, and other places of public accommodation had become integrated.[2]

The movement to abolish racial discrimination spread like wildfire throughout the country, especially in the South, and the walls of racial segregation began to crumble. The March on Washington was heralded as the event that would unify and further expand the movement.

HARDING: The leaders of civil rights groups, such as the National Association for the Advancement of Coloured People, the Congress of Racial Equality, the Southern Christian Leadership Conference and the Student Nonviolent Coordinating Committee, discussed the issue. Members of the Kennedy administration were included in the conversations, and at that point, the concept of the event changed.

The freedom movement up to that time was characterized by sit-ins, Freedom Rides and the protest marches of the Birmingham campaign. The Kennedy administration's response to the freedom movement, following the advice of leaders in the black community, was to draw up a civil rights bill, applicable to the entire United States, addressing all areas of public life, such as housing, education, public accommodations, other facilities, transportation and the voting booth.

The administration's policy was to enact laws that would create the means to ban racial segregation in the South and the entire nation. But President Kennedy and members of his administration were convinced that if an event as radical as a March on Washington were held, this would be used as ammunition by forces opposed to civil rights legislation.

IKEDA: Many leaders were concerned that by holding such a massive demonstration, violence might erupt and then sabotage the chances of enacting the civil rights legislation that seemed so close to becoming reality.

Leaders are always confronted with the choice of moving forward immediately or waiting for an opportune moment. Dr King described the deliberations on the march: 'It took daring and boldness to embrace the idea. The debate on the proposal neatly polarized positions.'[3] He was being pressed to make a difficult decision.

HARDING: Many persons were fearful that a massive March on Washington that drew thousands upon thousands of black people and their allies would invite violence by a small segment of the marchers. Therefore, the Kennedy administration and some of the more conservative black leaders proposed to feature King and some of the most conservative black leaders in a brief appearance, after which the gathering – which they hoped would be smaller than originally envisioned – would quickly disperse.

This general idea was the one that was eventually agreed upon. It was still called the 'March on Washington' and was still essentially meant to be a mobilization of people for an unprecedented gathering.

But when people, including thousands of white allies, streamed into Washington, DC, from every part of the country – by bus, plane, train and car – to express their solidarity with the freedom movement and their support for national civil rights legislation, the march become a larger and much more substantial event than the Kennedy administration and conservative black leaders had counted on. The enthusiastic commitment of the people overran the most cautious approaches of the leaders. Fortunately, there was no violence.

IKEDA: This day will always be regarded as a shining moment in the history of the movement for racial equality. Some 250,000 people filled the National Mall from the Washington Monument to the Lincoln Memorial. It was reported that a fifth of the participants were white. Burning with idealism for a just society that would transcend racial differences, everyone gathered proudly, a powerful sight telling of the triumph of the non-violent movement.

One of the marchers, just sixteen at the time and now an SGI-USA member, recalls:

> It was such a hot day. Thanks to my parents, I had developed a keen interest in the civil rights movement during my childhood, and so I was absolutely thrilled about being a part of the March on Washington.

In front of the Lincoln Memorial, the leaders of the civil rights movement took the rostrum to speak, the crowd cheering and clapping enthusiastically at every opportunity. Dr King movingly described this experience: 'The enormous multitude was the living, beating heart of an infinitely noble movement.'[4]

Where were you during this time?

HARDING: On the day of the march, I was at a meeting of academics at the University of Notre Dame. However, I watched the event on television with my colleagues at the conference.

Whatever we originally had in mind when we first started conceptualizing the march, seeing such a grand spectacle – thousands upon thousands of like-minded people gathered together, all seeking a new reality and sensing the tremendous vitality of their combined energy – was exciting and inspiring.

The Joy of Awakening to Our Infinite Potential

IKEDA: Having committed yourself completely to the success of the movement, this must have been all the more moving for you. The last of the many speakers to ascend the stage was Dr King. Standing in front of the massive white columns of the Lincoln Memorial and recalling the long history of hardships that had led the movement to this point, he proclaimed, 'Now is the time to rise from the dark and desolate valley of segregation to the sunlit path of racial justice.'[5]

Dr King shared his vision of an American society based on the ideals of peaceful coexistence: 'I have a dream that one day on the red hills of Georgia the sons of former slaves and the sons of former slave owners will be able to sit down together at the table of brotherhood.'[6] Through the media of television and radio, millions of people around the world heard Dr King's speech and were moved.

HARDING: The domestic and international response was enormous. It is interesting to note, and this is not well known, that King had given a similar speech about two months earlier at a major civil rights gathering in Detroit, Michigan, on 23 June 1963. His Washington speech was based on the earlier one, but he ad-libbed new elements – for example, the part about the 'red hills of Georgia', which was meant for the people who had gathered there from the South and had experienced the most violent opposition to the movement.

King spent a significant amount of his Washington speech outlining the difficulties that black people were experiencing in America, including poverty, police brutality, segregation in housing and bad schools. This aspect of King's speech has been completely forgotten. Only by taking seriously the long list of grievances that he presented can we understand the profound hope of his message, a hope in America that allowed him to say, 'I still have a dream.' This is the true significance of his dream, that he held on to it in the midst of harsh opposition and was willing to carry on this struggle – with his allies – to make the dream a reality.

IKEDA: It was a noble moment in history. Dr King acknowledged that the long, cruel history of racial discrimination, together with the harsh realities of the day, could not be overcome immediately, while he urged people to join him in advancing toward realizing the dream of a much brighter future. Dr King warned, 'If you lose hope, somehow you lose the vitality that keeps life moving, you lose that courage to be, that quality that helps you go on in spite of it all.'[7]

In the face of difficult circumstances, an effective leader must calmly, decisively instil hope and courage in people. King knew, I believe, that inside all people is hidden – even to themselves – great intrinsic potential and strength.

The Buddhist scriptures teach that all people are precious entities possessing inner wisdom and courage that can empower them to triumph over every hardship and enable their unique potential to shine with unparalleled brilliance.

A well-known story in the Lotus Sutra is the parable of the jewel in the robe: An impoverished man is invited to dinner at his wealthy friend's house, where he gets drunk and falls asleep. The friend has to rush out to take care of an urgent matter, but before he does, he sews a jewel of unequalled splendour into the lining of the sleeping man's robe. Unaware of the priceless jewel, the man embarks on a journey, drifting from country to country. When the man, by chance, meets up with his old friend again, the friend is surprised at the man's poverty-stricken appearance. The friend tells the man about the jewel he had sewn into his robe, and the man is overcome with joy and gratitude.

This parable shows, in simple terms, the principle that every human is endowed with the Buddha nature of infinite potential and inestimable worth. It teaches us that the key to overcoming the constraints of our present reality, whatever they may be, lies within ourselves.

HARDING: The parable of the jewel in the robe is a clear and compelling parable that tells us that no matter how wonderful a gift we have, if we are not aware of it, we cannot draw upon it for strength when necessary. Perhaps that is why I continue to urge my fellow American citizens to recognize the likelihood that our newly developing multiracial identity is a gift for us and the world.

IKEDA: A key condition for the continuity and development of any movement or any society is the joyful awakening of its people to their infinite potential. The March on Washington, the iconic moment of the freedom movement, was an opportunity to convey the movement's message of building a humane society – a message of vision and hope – to people all over the world.

HARDING: What I find most striking about King's speech is his assertion that 'even though we face the difficulties of today and tomorrow, I still have a dream'. The significance of his statement goes far beyond the rhetoric or oratorical skill with which it was delivered. It illustrates his inner struggle to maintain a sense of hope for America, even in the face of all the misdeeds and injustices heaped upon black people. Indeed, we still find it hard to create settings in which the 'sons [and daughters] of former slaves and the sons [and daughters] of former slave owners will be able to sit down together at the table of brotherhood',[8] to discover that they are brothers and sisters.

Speaking to the 250,000 people assembled there on the National Mall and an audience of millions all around the world, King's difficult challenge was to accurately portray the painful story of the past and present while also demonstrating faith in the magnificent possibilities for the future. King admonished his listeners to acknowledge this moment in 1963 not as an endpoint but as a new beginning in the ongoing struggle for a transformed America.

It is tempting to latch onto the concept of 'the dream' and leave the past behind, but to become mature as a nation, we need to honestly acknowledge the past on both a personal and collective level. We must not be overcome by the past but must deal with it with utmost honesty and, at the same time, embrace a hopeful view of the future. This is the only way that the dream can be meaningful and authentic as we continue to create a new present that leads to a transformed future.

IKEDA: A Buddhist text, the Contemplation on the Mind-Ground Sutra, contains this famous verse:

> If you want to understand the causes that existed in the past, look at the results as they are manifested in the present. And if you want to understand what results will be manifested in the future, look at the causes that exist in the present.[9]

To create a better future, we must examine the past and, at the same time, consider how to act in the present. This is the question constantly before us.

The twentieth century was undeniably a period of war and violence, and far too many people were victimized, their human dignity trampled underfoot. Unfortunately, this situation persists to this day.

The people of the twenty-first century must work tirelessly, with optimism and hope, so that our nations will mature as entities of cooperation and peace, and a mature global society can be created. This is the responsibility that each of us alive today must bear.

Religion should play an important role in helping us to achieve this goal.

At the end of this momentous day, 28 August, President Benjamin Mays of Morehouse College offered the closing prayer, thus drawing the curtain on one of the nation's most historic events. Recalling that Mays had also been president in King's Morehouse days, I sense in his participation that we were witnessing the culmination of a beautiful mentor–student relationship.

HARDING: King indeed began his journey on the path of non-violence largely as a result of the influence of President Mays (see Conversation Six). I believe in the fundamental truth that we can most experience the full richness of divine love through our relationships with others. Whether it is in our relationships with our family, teachers, colleagues or peers, we can experience the love of God in the richness of all these human relationships. Ultimately, it is through relationships that we discover our highest potential and are nurtured, shaped and opened to new possibilities. The mentor–student relationship is certainly one beautiful avenue of self-discovery.

Life, Death and Poetry

IKEDA: The mentor–student relationship lies at the core of any successful endeavour.

After the March on Washington, the freedom movement continued to expand vigorously throughout the country. But in response, the forces opposing its aims also became increasingly vehement. As we touched on earlier (see Conversation One), in mid-September 1963, only a few weeks after the march, a terrible incident took place: A Baptist church in Birmingham was bombed, and four young girls were killed. The church had been a point of assembly and departure for protestors during the Birmingham demonstrations.

At the funeral, Dr King delivered his 'Eulogy for the Martyred Children', in which he sought to comfort the grieving families and community. He offered profoundly compassionate words of solace and encouragement to the survivors and a poetic prayer for the repose of the young victims' souls. We can glimpse Dr King's perspective on life and death in the eulogy:

> Death is not a period that ends the great sentence of life, but a comma that punctuates it to more lofty significance. Death is not a blind alley that leads the human race into a state of nothingness, but an open door that leads man into life eternal. Let this daring faith, this great invincible surmise, be your sustaining power during these trying days.[10]

HARDING: King was influenced far more by philosophical ideas than by theological concepts. He was a person who understood the importance of the unity of all humankind and all life itself. It was also completely understandable that he would choose to see life and death in the context of a continuum, rather than as fragmented segments.

So many of the stories of where we come from and where we go from here are grounded in love and creativity. So, it was natural for King, who took life and love so seriously, to view life in this way.

And, of course, it is important to recognize that ultimately the only way that we can most fully talk about life or death is in poetry. King was in many ways a poet who loved the poetic expression of life.

I do not recall having any significant conversations with Martin about this matter of the transition from life into death. But King's statements that you quoted certainly reveal his natural appreciation of the continuity of life and are in accordance with his understanding of the continuity of God.

IKEDA: In his eulogy for the children, Dr King directly addressed the sorrow of the family and friends: 'In spite of the darkness of this hour, we must not despair. We must not become bitter, nor must we harbour the desire to retaliate with violence.'[11] Dr King expressed hope that the 'death of these little children may lead our whole Southland from the low road of man's inhumanity to man to the high road of peace and brotherhood'.[12]

To discover rays of hope, even in the darkest despair – this surely demonstrates the tenacious, indomitable conviction that enabled Dr King to dedicate his entire life to his noble cause. His philosophy of hope was unshakable, as solid as a rock.

HARDING: Not long ago, as a participant in a powerful seminar at the Ikeda Centre for Peace, Learning and Dialogue,[13] I shared some of my personal experiences of dealing with death. This was important for me in the sense that I never before had taken the opportunity to contemplate deeply the meaning of death. In my exploration of death, one of the most important things that became clear to me was that I have lived a rich life, full of many, many gifts that I could not ever have imagined. So, it would be natural to assume that the continuity of life and death is not just the continuity of experience but the continuity of the quality of the experience.

An understanding I gained from that Ikeda Centre gathering was that, just as I am grateful for the kind of life that I've been given, I will probably be grateful for the kind of death that I will be given as well. Somehow, the recognition of that continuity was a source of great joy for me.

IKEDA: In a lecture that I delivered at Harvard University in September 1993,[14] I spoke on the theme of life and death, and shared the wisdom of Buddhism, which recognizes joy in both life and death. At the end of our lives, the most important question will not be how long we have lived but rather how well we have lived. Those who have lived a fulfilling, joyful life will be surrounded by limitless joy upon their death. I have witnessed the inspiring life journeys of many people who have died in this way. Even those who die in unexpected accidents or natural disasters retain the 'treasures of the heart'[15] that they have accumulated through living a good, decent life.

To experience a 'good death', we must live a good life. I believe in the kind of good life in which we take action for and dedicate ourselves to the happiness of others. In Buddhism, this altruistic life is called the bodhisattva way. Living in this way gives us the power to transform the four sufferings of birth, aging, sickness and death into the abundant joy of the four virtues of eternity, happiness, true self and purity. Herein lies the purpose of our Buddhist faith. I am convinced that the honourable way in which you live your life and the way Dr King lived his exemplify the noble bodhisattva way.

Returning to our topic, it was on 2 July 1964, the year following the March on Washington, that President Johnson signed the Civil Rights Act of 1964 into law, and he and Dr King commemorated the event with a historic handshake. It was a victory that came as the nation was recovering from the tragedy of President Kennedy's assassination the previous November.

Dr King kept a demanding schedule, travelling all over the country and the world, continuing to advocate a philosophy of non-violence in the movement for social justice. That autumn, he had to be hospitalized for exhaustion. This was when Dr King received notice that he had been awarded the Nobel Peace Prize – an indication that his contribution to the non-violent struggle against racial discrimination had been recognized and applauded.

HARDING: I remember that when we first heard rumours that King was being considered for the Nobel Peace Prize, there was intense resistance in the white community in Atlanta and the rest of the South. For King to be publicly, internationally recognized in this way would, of course, be a judgement on the opponents of the black freedom movement – a clear message that he was right, and they were wrong. Indeed, the prize meant that the world recognized Martin as much more than an American hero.

Even as the day approached for King to travel to Sweden to receive the award, an ongoing debate took place in Atlanta about whether a special celebration should be held upon his return. So, what was good news for us was not received as such by everyone. Ultimately, Atlanta city officials came to realize that this was an honour of which the city should be proud. A native of their city had become a hero honoured by the world.

IKEDA: In his Nobel Peace Prize acceptance speech, Dr King spoke about the award as a recognition not just of himself but of the movement. He emphasized that he was accepting it on behalf of all the courageous people who helped develop and spread the movement and its philosophy of non-violence.

Dr King expressed his appreciation: 'Every time I take a flight I am always mindful of the many people who make a successful journey possible, the known pilots and the unknown ground crew.'[16] He shared his thoughts about those who quietly supported the endeavour from behind the scenes: 'You honor the ground crew without whose labor and sacrifices the jet flights to freedom could never have left the earth.'[17] This was typical of Dr King, who always retained his allegiance to the people, made their concerns his own, and fought on their behalf.

After Dr King received the Nobel Peace Prize, the movement evolved in the complex social and political context surrounding the Vietnam War.

CONVERSATION ELEVEN

Beyond Vietnam

IKEDA: On 2 December 1964, I penned the opening words of my lifework, my novel *The Human Revolution*: 'Nothing is more barbarous than war. Nothing is more cruel.'[1]

In the 1960s, the Vietnam War was engulfing Indochina. The number of US soldiers deployed to Vietnam rose dramatically, from 60,000 in 1965 to well over 540,000 in 1969, and the casualties continued to rise as the war evolved into an ever-deepening tragedy. On 4 April 1967, with the devastating consequences of the war increasingly obvious, Dr King took bold, decisive action by delivering a historic speech, titled 'Beyond Vietnam', in which he asserted his opposition to the Vietnam War. Let's discuss Dr King's speech and explore his resolve and the struggles he faced, as well as the important role that you played in drafting the speech.

HARDING: To begin, in those days, King wrestled with the issue of how and when to make an even more public statement about his views on the Vietnam War than he had made in 1963 and 1964. He decided that he did not want to simply become absorbed into the national anti-war movement. He wanted to make clear that his opposition to the war was based on a religious and spiritual consciousness, and that it came from the principled position of a person who had devoted himself to transforming the country and making it a more democratic place.

King knew that he would probably be subject to harsh criticisms. He thought this because in the mid-1960s, the anti-war movement had still not garnered much public support or achieved the degree of intensity and strength that it did later. Domestic opinion – as evidenced by newspaper editorials and columns, and the views of intellectuals, politicians and other leaders – still supported the war.

IKEDA: Not everyone today may grasp the perilous circumstances under which Dr King courageously stepped forward to make this speech. I experienced the social climate of that era, so I understand what enormous courage he had.

The US involvement in the war was motivated by the belief, called the 'domino theory', that if one country fell to communism, then neighbouring countries would all collapse and turn to communism, just like a cascade of falling dominoes. The assertion was that the advance of communism, which had swept through the USSR, China and North Vietnam, must be stopped in South Vietnam.

The United States supported the ruling Ngo Dinh Diem regime of South Vietnam, which turned out to be a nepotistic dictatorship that proceeded to strengthen its hold on power and brutally oppress all opponents by accusing them of being communists. After a successful coup d'état, Duong Van Minh became president, and the conflict between the South Vietnam government and the Vietnamese National Liberation Front (the Viet Cong) worsened. In the midst of this Vietnamese domestic strife, the United States became more involved.

HARDING: One of the most important issues King had to deal with was the fact that President Johnson had essentially made the war his own and, under his leadership, it had become synonymous with him. The main dilemma was that the Texas-born President Johnson recognized, perhaps more than any other US president, the necessity for a resolution to race problems in this country. He understood that any reforms required what he called a 'war on poverty'. Accordingly, in many ways, the freedom movement considered Johnson an ally, and Johnson considered himself an ally and supporter of the movement.

IKEDA: President Johnson was sworn in following President Kennedy's assassination and inherited and carried on Kennedy's civil rights policies. The legislation that Dr King and other civil rights leaders had hoped and worked for, such as the Civil Rights Act of 1964 and the Voting Rights Act of 1965, was enacted during President Johnson's tenure. Yet President Johnson also forcefully pressed forward with the Vietnam War, which turned into a desperate quagmire.

Therefore, to proclaim opposition to the Vietnam War would put Dr King in direct conflict with President Johnson, the president who had expressed such sympathy with the civil rights movement.

HARDING: At a time when the Vietnam War was increasingly being called 'Johnson's War', King knew that if he came out publicly against the war, Johnson might take it personally. However, King also knew in his heart that he could not stay silent. He knew that he must speak out about the serious injustices that he saw in the United States and in Vietnam.

IKEDA: As Vietnam continued to be ravaged by war, the Japanese government supported the United States in the bombing of North Vietnam, but opposition to the Vietnam War was widespread among the Japanese public. I was moved to respond. In November 1966, I spoke in front of 15,000 youth and, expressing my convictions as a Buddhist and my commitment to peace, called for the immediate end of the Vietnam War and the withdrawal of US forces. I also called on the Japanese government to convene an international peace conference in Tokyo and submit a plan to the United Nations to bring about a concrete resolution to the conflict. I made the same appeal the following year and again the year after that. In 1968, when I made my proposal for the normalization of Japan's diplomatic relations with China, I again called for an end to the Vietnam conflict and for peace and stability in Asia.

Furthermore, I sent a letter, dated 1 January 1973, to President Richard Nixon, President Johnson's successor, with a detailed proposal for a peaceful resolution. It was a long letter; translated, it was thirty-eight pages of English text. Through an intermediary, it was arranged that US National Security Advisor Henry Kissinger would deliver the letter to President Nixon. Dr Kissinger was playing a key role in the Vietnam peace talks. Two years later, in January 1975, I met with him in Washington, DC, and we have stayed in contact ever since.

I fervently prayed and earnestly wished for a swift end to the war, which inflicted so much suffering on the Vietnamese people and stole the lives of so many young people.

HARDING: Thanks, my dear brother, for sharing with me this powerful account of your long and important opposition to the Vietnam War. It draws you and my beloved brother Martin together. Your concerns and motivations for opposition were very similar to his. As a pastor, King understood that continuation of the war inflicted injury on the poor people of both countries and was ultimately damaging to our souls and our spirit. His desire to speak out was from a love and concern for America and its people as well as for the people of Vietnam.

In the course of our friendship, King and I often discussed the war and its many destructive and unjustifiable aspects. We had many discussions on the topic, and we understood each other.

In 1965, my wife and I left the South and returned to Chicago, where I continued working on my dissertation. Almost immediately after I finished the dissertation, I accepted a position as chairperson of the history department at Spelman College in Atlanta. But I decided that I could not go to Spelman, or any place else to teach, unless I had a much deeper understanding of the history and significance of the Vietnam War. As a result, I chose the twentieth anniversary of the bombing of Hiroshima to begin a tremendous amount of research on the origins of the war, starting with the experience of French colonialism, the attempt of the Vietnamese to free themselves from French rule, and all the factors involved in the subsequent US support of French colonial policy.

At the time, my wife and I were involved in the life and work of the Mennonite church (see Conversation Four). My views on war in general and that war in particular were influenced by my Mennonite connections.

IKEDA: So, these were the circumstances that led Dr King to entrust you with the task of drafting his anti-Vietnam War speech.

HARDING: Also, in the summer of 1965, King's organization, the Southern Christian Leadership Conference, was meeting in Birmingham. I was still in Chicago and, although I usually attended the meetings, this time I was unable to, so I sent an open letter to King and the meeting attendees. In essence, I urged the attendees to remember that our freedom movement had welcomed worldwide support and solidarity from people of colour and people suffering the effects of colonialism across the globe. I pointed out that now, when our own country was acting like a colonial power, we could not be silent in the face of this injustice, especially given the way that colonized people had stood with us.

In my letter, I called upon the SCLC to support what I knew to be King's growing desire for the organization to be more open in its opposition. I encouraged the participants to make a joint statement opposing the war.

That year, President Johnson, who had heard about King's early opposition to the war, arranged for him to meet with Arthur Goldberg, the US ambassador to the United Nations. Johnson wanted King to meet with Ambassador Goldberg because he was sure that, as he put it, the ambassador could 'set King straight' and explain to him why he should support the war. Martin asked me to prepare some talking points for him for the meeting. He asked me partly because of the letter that I had written and also because of our previous discussions about the war.

IKEDA: This shows how much Dr King trusted you. And it is this behind-the-scenes careful planning and cooperation that provided the impetus for his historic speech.

HARDING: A request for Martin to speak on the issue of the war came sometime in the fall of 1966 from an organization of clergy and lay people concerned about Vietnam. They asked him to speak at Riverside Church in New York, famous for its leading role in social justice.

King felt that this invitation presented the perfect opportunity to make a full statement to a large, religiously based audience. This would not be just a statement of his opposition to the war, it would be a thorough explanation of why he opposed the war as an American, as a Christian and as a compassionate human being.

Maintaining a backbreaking travel schedule, King knew that he did not have the time to devote to preparing a speech that would express his thoughts to his satisfaction. Again, he realized that this was an important opportunity for him to fully say what he wanted to say. It was in this context that he asked me to draft the speech for him.

He probably thought that a college professor would have more time than he had. I guess he was right, but I could not get to it until the holidays, when my students at Spelman College were on vacation. Fortunately, during the Christmas holidays, I had no classes, and my wife was planning to take our two children to visit family in Chicago. So, I had time alone to work on the draft.

IKEDA: In January of the following year (1967), conditions were worsening. In his budget message, President Johnson proposed a tax increase to expand the Vietnam War.

Were there any points that Dr King wanted to emphasize in the speech?

HARDING: Actually, no. The most important goal for me was not to write what I thought King should say but to take what I understood to be his thinking and put it into words. He had asked me to do the draft simply because I had the time to develop the speech, and he did not. There was no need for him to request a particular emphasis because we were of one heart and mind about what was occurring. So, I simply wrote what I knew to be in his heart.

Andrew Young was our go-between. When I finished the draft, I turned it over to Andrew, and he gave it to Martin, who shared it with several others, made some additions, especially in the last part, and that was it.

THE POOR FIGHTING THE POOR

IKEDA: As you have put it, the speech was not simply a refutation of the Vietnam War but included the fundamentals for building a wholesome America and having compassion for the Vietnamese people's welfare.

HARDING: As you no doubt know, the US government was at that time still conducting the military draft. Most of the young people drafted and sent to Vietnam had not had the opportunity for a higher education. The majority were youth not in college or not employed in what were considered 'significant jobs', and they needed work. This reality was clear.

King viewed this problem as a pastor would, rather than as a politician might. He felt it was a great wrong for a country to treat its poorest youth in this way.

IKEDA: In 1990, I spoke in Tokyo with Director Kevin Bowen and board member Robert Glassman of the William Joiner Centre for the Study of War and Social Consequences at the University of Massachusetts. The centre, well known for its research on the Vietnam War, is named after William Joiner, an African-American Vietnam veteran who died of cancer related to Agent Orange, the defoliant used in Vietnam.

At my meeting with Mr Bowen and Mr Glassman, both of whom had served in Vietnam, they mentioned the striking statistic that, despite being around 11 per cent of the entire US population at that time, African Americans made up more than 50 per cent of those on the front lines in the Vietnam War.

HARDING: This was the reality. King discerned that likewise among the Vietnamese, those who suffered the most were the poor, the farmers and the labourers. This whole drama of sending the poor to fight the poor was a terrible injustice.

In addition to this, King was clear that the money used to carry out the war was money taken away from addressing the needs of the poor in our country.

IKEDA: King mentioned the Vietnamese Proclamation of Independence from French imperial control, declared in 1945 at the end of World War II, in the 'Beyond Vietnam' speech. The beginning of the proclamation borrows a passage from the Declaration of Independence: 'All men are created equal' and are 'endowed by their Creator with certain unalienable rights'.

HARDING: In 1775, America legitimized its independence on this basis, presenting what should be a common truth of humankind. Even so, the United States ignored its Declaration of Independence, turning its back on its most sacred principles and refusing to recognize the Vietnamese call for assistance in its attempt to gain independence from its French colonial controllers.

IKEDA: In the speech, Dr King unleashed a scathing critique of America's position, lamenting that 'we again fell victim to the deadly Western arrogance that has poisoned the international atmosphere for so long'.[2] It is moving how pained Dr King was, knowing that millions of dollars in US military spending were being used to victimize innocent Asians, while in the United States, many people were suffering from discrimination and poverty.

At the beginning of 1966, Dr King rented an apartment in the slums of Chicago and saw the depth of poverty and despair in which black people in the northern states lived. The North did not have the explicit Jim Crow laws that existed in the South, but the social structure and the educational system amplified the inequities and left many young blacks with a profound sense of powerlessness.

Dr King tried to convince the alienated, despairing youth he met that Molotov cocktails and guns would not solve anything. The youth demanded answers to their questions, asking pointedly: 'What about Vietnam? Isn't our country solving its problems using massive American military force?'

King knew that the issues the youth were raising were right on the mark. He realized that he could not teach these alienated youth about non-violence without first addressing the violence and immense destructive power of the US military being inflicted on the small Southeast Asian country of Vietnam. Perhaps Dr King's anti-war declaration was meant to address, in part, the young people's sense of rage and frustration at injustice.

HARDING: Yes, these young Americans were very much on our mind. Around that time, youth in the black communities in the United States were bursting with a sense of injustice, frustration and anger. They were burning their own neighbourhoods.

What we were saying in the speech was this: What sense did it make to tell young black people to be non-violent when confronted by southern sheriffs and northern police trying to kill them but to be violent toward Vietnamese peasants who had nothing against them at all?

We also meant to address the criticisms from within the civil rights movement that urged us not to mix the civil rights and anti-war movements. It was clear to Martin that he was well-respected in the country and around the world, and that for him to remain silent about what his country was doing would be wrong.

Silence Is Betrayal

IKEDA: This is why Dr King was a great man. He was determined that his conscience would guide his actions, never calculating the political benefit or letting concerns for his personal safety overwhelm him.

Dr King wrote:

> On some positions, Cowardice asks the question, 'Is it safe?' Expediency asks the question, 'Is it politic?' And Vanity comes along and asks the question, 'Is it popular?'

> But Conscience asks the question, 'Is it right?' And there comes a time when one must take a position that is neither safe, nor politic, nor popular, but he must do it because Conscience tells him it is right.[3]

This statement shows that Dr King's chosen way of life emanated from his religious faith.

HARDING: Whenever the question comes up about why King broke his silence and spoke out against the war, we are reminded of the prophets of the Old Testament as well as those of other religious traditions. None of them could remain silent when faced with terrible injustice.

King even said so himself. He could not remain silent and felt moved to raise his voice. To continue to remain silent would have been unthinkable for him. His faith compelled him to speak out. Even if he had to stand alone, he was prepared to suffer the consequences. As he stated at the beginning of the Vietnam speech, 'A time comes when silence is betrayal.'[4]

IKEDA: Few people have the courage to stand up for what they believe, especially when they are alone in their belief. One person unwavering in her commitment to peace was Jeannette Rankin, the first woman to become a member of the US House of Representatives. It is well known that in December 1941, when US nationalistic fervour peaked after the Japanese attack on Pearl Harbor, Rankin cast the sole vote opposing the US entry into World War II.[5]

In 1968, Representative Rankin joined Coretta Scott King in speaking out against the Vietnam War and in leading women in protests and marches against the war. Rankin's firm commitment to peace and non-violence was based on Mahatma Gandhi's philosophy.

Gandhi made this oft-quoted statement:

> The greatest men of the world have always stood alone. Take the great prophets, Zoroaster, Buddha, Jesus, Mohammad – they all stood alone like many others who I can name.[6]

All the founders of the world's great religions engaged in principled action based on the desire for peace and happiness for all people. My mentor often emphasized returning to this original purpose and believed that a 'common understanding would be achieved if the original teachers of the major religions – Nichiren, Shakyamuni, Jesus Christ and Muhammad – all got together in one room and held a conference'.[7]

In the same way, underpinning Dr King's courage to be the lone voice for non-violent struggle was a profound philosophy whose elevated spiritual vantage point enabled him to see beyond the petty differences that divide humanity and to seek to transform society.

HARDING: As King declared in his speeches and sermons, we are all children of God. This expressed his profound conviction, and it meant that there was no way that he could support war as a means of conflict resolution.

He insisted on the fundamental principle that war was not in accord with God's will. As a follower of Jesus Christ and the philosophy of Gandhi, he could not accept war as a means to right injustice. As King repeatedly explained, war brings in its wake even more evil, and rather than resolving wrongs, it amplifies them many times over.

IKEDA: The Vietnam War killed more than a million and caused irreparable harm to countless others. This tragedy affected people of every generation, and it continues to inflict suffering even today.[8]

Once begun, war ushers in irreversible tragedy and untold misery. This is why people of faith all over the world must stand up courageously, as Dr King did, and contribute to building peace, mutual understanding and friendship and solidarity among all the world's peoples. For many years, based on this conviction, the Soka Gakkai International has been a grassroots movement spreading peace, culture and education throughout the world.

In our next conversation, let's explore the reverberations from Dr King's anti-Vietnam War speech and its influence on society and the spirit of the times.

CONVERSATION TWELVE

A Revolution of Values

IKEDA: At the height of the Vietnam War, when students of Vietnam National University, Hanoi, were forced to take refuge in bomb shelters, they studied by the light of fireflies they collected in glass bottles. This historical detail was shared with me when I welcomed VNU President Dao Trong Thi and his party to Soka University in Tokyo (September 2005). Indeed, education is the light that pierces the darkness of ignorance and despair, and radiates human dignity.

VNU was the first Vietnamese educational institution to seek exchange with American universities, making a major contribution to the restoration of diplomatic relations between Vietnam and the United States (1995).

The Vietnam War lasted for fifteen years, beginning in 1960 and ending in 1975, leaving in its wake deep, deep scars in the hearts of both Americans and Vietnamese. I find it significant that education has played an important role in opening the way to friendly relations between the two countries.

It was with the fervent conviction that the twenty-first century must be a century in which education triumphs and peace reigns supreme that, joined by young Soka University alumni, I welcomed President Thi and his group. Our discussion touched on Dr King and the way that he courageously stood up, raising his voice against the Vietnam War. When Dr King delivered his historic anti-war speech, it immediately struck a chord in the hearts of people all across America and, indeed, throughout the world.

HARDING: A friend involved in the anti-Vietnam War movement told me that the Vietnamese were impressed when they read the text of this statement, especially that it included so much of the history of their struggle against colonialism. They began considering how this might affect their response to the black soldiers there in the American forces.

King was aware of the many constituencies in the audience to which he was speaking. He especially directed his message to religious progressives. They were appreciative that King had spoken out against the war. This was because King's speech not only expressed opposition to the Vietnam War, it also provided the basis for the religious case against the war and for a new direction in the way the United States should engage with the world.

There is no way to determine how much impact the speech had on ending the war. However, it did provide much support for people searching for a spiritual and religious foundation for their opposition to the war. It helped people in the freedom movement make the connection between what we were doing and the need to raise our voices against the war. It inspired courage in people.

IKEDA: On the other hand, a great many people reacted sharply against Dr King's speech, expressing open, emphatic disapproval. Those criticisms were so intense that, at one point, Dr King wrote: 'When I first took my position against the war in Vietnam, almost every newspaper in the country criticized me. It was a low period in my life.'[1]

By taking a stand against the war, Dr King had placed himself in an even more perilous situation – a situation that led to increased threats on his life and to his becoming an even greater target of the surveillance and wiretapping that had been used against him for years by government authorities.

HARDING: Martin expected his speech to draw opposition from many quarters, but he was surprised by how much there was, especially from those in the black freedom movement. He later wrote that many of the people critical were some of the most conservative members of the movement. They were fearful of what they called 'mixing' civil rights and anti-war issues together. They were concerned that connecting the issues of the two movements would not only jeopardize the freedom movement's relationship with President Johnson but also endanger relationships with white liberal fundraisers and donors.

IKEDA: I have heard that, at the time, internationally prominent leaders of the black movement were among those who expressed concern about Dr King's anti-war declaration. Dr King received criticism even from long-time friends. And the National Association for the Advancement of Colored People, an organization that Dr King had worked with in the movement, released a public statement criticizing his speech.

HARDING: There was indeed immense opposition. *The New York Times*, in its 7 April 1967, editorial, said that King had

> linked his personal opposition to the war in Vietnam with the cause of Negro equality in the United States . . . This is a fusing of two public problems that are distinct and separate. By drawing them together, Dr King has done a disservice to both.

The *Washington Post* expressed a similar criticism. But that was all the more reason it was so important that Martin knew exactly what he needed to do and why, no matter the consequences. Martin knew well how risky and hazardous it was for him to speak out against the war in such an absolutely public way. It was already clear that many keepers of the American status quo considered him a dangerous figure.

Around the time of the 'I Have a Dream' speech (29 August, 1963), the FBI, led by Director J. Edgar Hoover, labelled King the 'most dangerous Negro' in America.[2] The FBI was trying in a variety of ways to destroy him.

IKEDA: In 1967, throughout the country, many anti-war meetings and demonstrations were held. Dr Ronald A. Bosco, former president of The Thoreau Society, shared in our dialogue, published as *Creating Waldens*,[3] about almost being expelled from college for joining the demonstrations. Joel Myerson, who joined us in the same dialogue, also was a protester. Many youth shared a keen sense of the crisis gripping the times and began to speak out passionately.

In his anti-war speech, Dr King was critical of the moral posture of the country. He asserted, 'The war in Vietnam is but a symptom of a far deeper malady within the American spirit.'[4] Using the prior decade of US foreign policy as an example, Dr King blamed the situation on three injustices at the root of the problem.

HARDING: The three evils were racism, extreme materialism and militarism. And during the last two years of his life, King reiterated this message. It was not surprising at all that King's work, during what turned out to be his last years, was not limited to the issue of civil rights, not limited to a focus on the racism that denied so many Americans their civil and human rights.

He saw there was more to be done, and he proceeded to identify the 'woundedness of America' in terms of the deep psychological malaise caused by materialism. King saw what the emphasis on materialism was doing to American society – it had led us to create a society with a gaping divide between those at the top and the rest of society. It virtually guaranteed the existence of poverty.

King saw that by allowing this economic gap to develop, we had created a society that was completely contrary to the 'beloved community' that we all were seeking – a beloved community characterized by loving, caring relationships among all people. As the logical extension of this thought, King spoke to the issues of materialism and militarism.

IKEDA: What is particularly interesting to me is that Dr King explicitly stated in the speech that to resolve these deeply rooted social problems, 'we as a nation must undergo a radical revolution of values'.[5] To bring about this 'revolution of values', Dr King asserted that a rapid shift from a 'thing-oriented society' to a 'person-oriented society'[6] was essential. He astutely pointed out that giving priority to things over people gives rise to a coldhearted, ruthless society that dehumanizes people.

This transformation in our values – from a society in which things take precedence over people to one in which people take precedence over things – is the first step to peace and completely in accord with the ideals motivating our Soka Gakkai International movement for peace, culture and education.

HARDING: King discerned that militarism is a system of thought based on the assumption that we must build our security on the insecurity of others – that we achieve our goals through the destruction of others. This assumption is mistaken. Rather, it is important that we avoid building our security on the insecurity of others. To build our happiness on the unhappiness of others is to base our lives upon an unstable foundation.

That perspective was opposed to King's understanding of human beings as children of God. To King, being children of God meant that we do not live isolated and separate existences. Rather, it meant that, in order to create the 'beloved community', we must build a society that not only protects each person's civil rights but also enables people to relate to one another with love and compassion.

IKEDA: The idea that our security should not be based on the insecurity of others must be the foundation on which we build a society of peaceful coexistence.

In the late 1990s, the Ikeda Centre for Peace, Learning and Dialogue published a collection of essays titled *Subverting Hatred: The Challenge of Nonviolence in Religious Traditions*. This was followed, after the terrorist attacks of 11 September 2001, by *Subverting Greed: Religious Perspectives on the Global Economy*. In these publications, some of the world's leading intellectuals, representing various religions and disciplines, explored how those of differing religious, cultural and ethnic traditions can overcome hatred and redress poverty and economic injustice.

In the foreword to *Subverting Greed*, I emphasized that one cannot build one's happiness on the unhappiness of others. This is a fundamental philosophical truth of human life that I have consistently stressed in my talks with young people.

Buddhism teaches, again, that the Buddha nature is inherent in all people. A fundamental precept of Buddhist teachings is to honour the dignity and worth of our fellow human beings and of all life. The key is for people to transcend their differences and earnestly strive for others' happiness as well as their own. It is becoming increasingly urgent for people of faith to advocate building a society of peaceful coexistence founded on the principle of the sanctity of life.

Dr King pointed out the challenges of addressing social ills – the inhumanity and low regard for the sanctity of life that permeate modern society – and transforming our values. We could say that this struggle is a struggle against the ego, the self that lacks compassion.

HARDING: In Abraham Lincoln's terms, this is a battle between the better and worse angels of our nature.[7] The reason King was such a precious person is precisely the reason such precious people like him are often destroyed. They force us to look at the internal battle inside each of us.

Through their actions more than their words, these precious people insist that we decide what kind of human being we will be. Unfortunately, many of us are afraid that if we make such a decision, we will no longer be in control of our lives and will be forced to re-vision the way we think the world should be. So, we allow ourselves to be locked into ways of thinking and acting that drive us away from our best selves.

That fear of discovering our most compassionate, creative and vulnerable selves was an important part of what motivated the forces that brought about King's death. King challenged us to break away from the view that war was necessary to maintain and continue American society as we knew it at that time. The opposition was terrified of what would happen if a large number of people took King's words seriously and began to follow a new, life-affirming path. They perceived this possibility as a dire threat to their own reality and way of life.

In the same way, in those final years, there was a great fear of King's capacity to inspire the nation's varied poor people to come together in Washington, DC, and challenge our national leaders to turn from a war of imperialist power to a war against poverty. This was the original intent of the Poor People's Campaign.[8]

Too Young To Die

Ikeda: The Vietnam War, of course, continued after Dr King's speech, and the turmoil and confusion within the United States deepened. On 31 March of the following year (1968), President Johnson announced that he would not seek re-election and declared a unilateral cessation of the bombing of North Vietnam.

Then, on 4 April, exactly one year after his anti-war speech, Dr King, visiting Memphis, Tennessee, to support municipal sanitation workers striking for better working conditions, was shot by an assassin as he stood speaking with friends on his hotel balcony.

Dr King's assassination sent shock waves throughout the United States and around the world. How did you hear about Dr King's death?

Harding: On that day, Rosemarie and I were having dinner with a friend from New York. We were at Pascal's, a black-owned restaurant in Atlanta, where movement people often gathered. The owner of Pascal's knew us and our relationship with King well. He had heard the news on the radio and came over to our table to let us know.

In those days, there were of course no cell phones, so to try to find out what had happened, we left the restaurant hurriedly and went home to call friends. At first, we received word that King had been shot. Then, a few hours later, we learned that he had taken his last breath.

When the call came that King was dead, I felt an overwhelming sense of anger. I remember that I furiously banged my fists against the wall where the telephone was hanging.

Ikeda: Dr King was just thirty-nine; he was too young to die. His death was a great loss for America and humankind's future.

Leaders of the freedom movement lived each day knowing and

accepting the threat of death. Even so, the news of Dr King's assassination came as a terrible shock and plunged many people into deep sorrow. I am sure that no one can even imagine the complexity of your feelings then.

HARDING: For a long time, I felt a profound sense of anguish about my role in Martin's death – for I was certain that it was his impassioned call for an end to the war, for the organizing of the poor, and for a new American approach to the world that most directly led to his assassination.

As someone intimately involved in creating the text of his anti-Vietnam War speech, I anguished over my responsibility for what had happened. I don't even remember how long I struggled with those feelings; it must have been at least a year or maybe longer.

In the midst of my struggle, the Reverend James Lawson, a good friend who had also been close to Martin, helped me a great deal. He was the person who had invited King to Memphis. Sometime after the assassination, during a phone conversation with Lawson, I asked him how he felt about having played a role in bringing King to Memphis. I wanted to know if he felt any guilt about that.

IKEDA: I cannot even imagine the terrible anguish you must have felt over Dr King's death.

The Reverend James Lawson was the one organizing support for the sanitation workers' general strike, wasn't he? Mr Lawson had contacted Dr King to ask him to lead a demonstration march; Dr King had accepted the request and had gone to Memphis, where the tragedy occurred. How did Mr Lawson respond to your question?

HARDING: Jim is a wise person. He understood why I was asking my question. He responded by telling me an interesting story about the first time that he had asked King to come to Memphis.

Jim had phoned Martin and had asked him to come to Memphis to stand together with the sanitation workers.

The sanitation workers were convinced that they were not getting the attention they needed for their cause, but that if King were with them, he would help shine a light on their struggle because the media followed him everywhere he went.

4 April was the second time in short succession King went to Memphis. Jim called him about a week before, and apparently King was in a meeting because Jim heard voices in the background. Someone was calling out to him: 'Martin, we don't have time to go to Memphis. Tell Jim that you have other things to do. We're working on this Poor People's Campaign. You can't go!'

But King was determined to respond to the call of the garbage collectors. Despite the opposition from his staff, he went to Memphis. Even after an outbreak of violence seemed to abort his mission, King came back again, determined to lead a non-violent demonstration. And on the second visit, he was destroyed by violence.

It was clear to Jim that King wanted to go to Memphis. He wasn't forced or pressured into going, Jim assured me.

King was following his heart. Both times, his visits to Memphis were motivated by his desire to go there. Jim was not guilt-stricken like I was because, he said, it was King's own decision to go to Memphis; this was the place King wanted to be. My conversation with Jim was an enormous comfort to me. I realized that Martin was determined to speak out in opposition to the war, in support of the poor. I simply provided the words that belonged to both of us.

IKEDA: What a moving story. Dr King tried to pack as much into his schedule as possible. In those days, he would sometimes give up to thirty-five talks in one week. James Lawson must have known that it was Dr King's personal commitment that took him to Memphis, despite his hectic schedule.

Many people had already sensed that danger was closing in on Dr King, and rumours of assassination plots abounded. Even so, Dr King was not intimidated in the slightest. He boldly pushed forward on his courageous path.

For Dr King, raising his voice to protest the injustices of the Vietnam War was a natural response for anyone with a conscience and a sense of humanity. Going one step further, he agonized over how to build a peaceful world.

HARDING: It was clear to me that most of the vocabulary and phrases in King's anti-war speech were mine, but they came directly from his heart. We shared the same convictions, and my job was to make sure that the audience would grasp the meaning and significance of what he was saying and also have a firm understanding of the man and the spirit motivating his words.

A Life of Service

IKEDA: Buddhism teaches the concept of the 'oneness of life and death'. Spiritual comrades who live up to their noble missions are united as one across the boundaries of life and death. I strongly sense that you and Dr King share a deep, enduring, spiritual bond.

In his last speech, Dr King spoke of Mahatma Gandhi, assassinated in the midst of India's tumultuous struggle for human rights. In February 1959, Dr King received an invitation from Prime Minister Jawaharlal Nehru, and so he and Mrs King travelled to India and visited places that had been important in Gandhi's life.

I had the opportunity to visit Gandhi's resting place in Raj Ghat on two occasions and also visited Birla House – the Gandhi Memorial Hall – where Gandhi was assassinated. At the Memorial Hall, I met with Dr Neelakanta Radhakrishnan, director of the Memorial Hall, and Dr Bishambhar N. Pande, a leading disciple of

Gandhi. Dr Pande was incarcerated eight times, spending a total of ten years in prison, but continued to stand firmly as a champion of human rights.

I will never forget Dr Pande resolutely telling me that he would 'continue proclaiming the teachings of Gandhi until my eyes close forever on the very last day of my life'. Indeed, in keeping his word, Dr Pande continued to wage his non-violent campaigns.

Gandhi's philosophy was realized fully in the civil rights movement, thanks to the hard work and struggle of courageous individuals such as Dr King and you. No matter how great the philosophy or principle, if there is no one to carry on and implement the philosophy, the movement will be broken. This is why Dr King held such high expectations for the youth, just as Gandhi did.

As a colleague of Dr King and as one who shared his philosophy and convictions, what do you think is important to impress upon the youth of today?

HARDING: What people need to do is not so much to follow King as to explore and discover for themselves the sources of inspiration, hope and courage that gave King meaning in his life. Instead of focusing on King himself, if people would focus on what King focused on, they would tap into a more powerful source of strength and inspiration.

When I speak about King to young people, I try to help them understand that King was a child of a typical middle-class family in America that happened to be black in the South. King's family was a middle-class family like almost every other middle-class family – the major objective was to achieve a comfortable way of life. One of the constant refrains of the middle-class mentality was the desire of young families to achieve a higher economic status than their parents and for these new parents to hope that their own children would surpass them in material achievement.

King kept speaking to black young people and asking them

to consider what it was that would be meaningful in their lives. Would they gain more satisfaction by acquiring material benefits or by building the 'beloved community'?

As we look to King's life as a model and try to understand his philosophy, most revealing is the fact that he grew up in a typical middle-class setting – but one that was informed by his family's deep religious conviction that a full life was lived in service to the needy. So, he devoted himself to serving others.

At the end of his life, he was organizing a Poor People's Campaign, and he was assassinated while working with garbage workers to better their lives. Portraying King's life in this way provides a more striking perspective than perhaps anything we could say about his philosophy.

IKEDA: Standing alongside and acting for those suffering – this is the drama of Dr King's life. Nothing is more powerful than this.

Nichiren's writings contain this passage: 'More valuable than treasures in a storehouse are the treasures of the body, and the treasures of the heart are the most valuable of all.'[9] No matter how blessed with material possessions we may be, if we are poor in spirit and overcome by anger and ego, our lives will ultimately be filled with conflict, we will never be happy and we will fall into ruin. Only by winning out over such spiritual shortcomings and leading a life of service to others and society can we shine as people with the 'treasures of the heart' and experience true fulfilment and joy.

Such an effort is precisely what Dr King emphasized in his anti-Vietnam War speech and also what he based his life on – the transformation from a thing-oriented society to a person-oriented society; philosophy and action to create a society based on peaceful coexistence.

In one of the many unforgettable passages from the Riverside speech, he asserted:

> A genuine revolution of values means in the final analysis that our loyalties must become ecumenical rather than sectional. Every nation must now develop an overriding loyalty to mankind as a whole in order to preserve the best in their individual societies.[10]

The responsibility of our generation must be to foster a network of young people determined to live up to their noble mission and to engage in the challenge of inner transformation. They are global citizens motivated by a powerful loyalty to all humankind and devoted to contributing to peace on Earth.

HARDING: Again, perhaps the best way to summarize the way King lived his life is with four words: courage, commitment, creativity and compassion. These four words seem to encapsulate the essence of his life as a leader, a teacher and a pastor. We must all embody the spirit of these four qualities as we strive to build the 'beloved community' throughout the world.

CONVERSATION THIRTEEN

Non-violent Acts of Courage

IKEDA: In a September 1961 speech to the United Nations, President Kennedy declared, 'Mankind must put an end to war or war will put an end to mankind.'[1] Dr King quoted these words in his speeches, telling his audience: 'It is no longer a choice, my friends, between violence and non-violence. It is either non-violence or nonexistence.'[2] He emphasized that if we did not reject nuclear arms and militarism, 'our earthly habitat would be transformed into an inferno that even the mind of Dante could not imagine'.[3]

In spite of this alarm raised by Dr King, humanity chose to rush headlong into a pointless, insane arms race – a path that has endangered its very existence. At a terrifying pace far exceeding that during Dr King's lifetime, nuclear weapons are proliferating throughout the world, while new weapons of mass destruction and military technologies are being constantly developed.

At this time of impending crisis, how can humanity take up the torch of non-violence and build a peaceful society of coexistence on Earth? Meeting this challenge demands all of humanity's wisdom and capability.

What are your thoughts on building such a peaceful society?

Harding: Education has an essential role to play. The only way that we can carry on and expand upon the non-violent philosophy of Gandhi and King is to make it a central part of what we teach. It seems to me that most children and even adults have no idea that there are other ways of achieving justice besides resorting to the use of destructive force and retaliation. This is why it is so important that education provide a vision of an alternative way of life.

The World Social Forum, first held in 2001 in Porto Alegre, Brazil, has created the opportunity for people from grassroots movements all over the world to work together. The vision that emerged from the first gathering, and continues to be the dream and goal of the WSF on the international as well as regional levels, is expressed in the declaration that 'Another World is Possible'. This is the fundamental idea that informs all of my own endeavours.

No matter what form education may take – whether it be institutional or informal, religious or secular – I am convinced that one of its most important responsibilities is to nurture the realization that we can change our lives for the better, that another creative, more democratic way of life is possible, that the seeds of such a new way are already alive within us, needing to be nurtured.

Ikeda: In the twentieth century, war and violence combined with the astonishing development of science and technology to claim an unprecedented number of victims. Furthermore, attempts at radical social change produced totalitarianism steeped in mass violence, in complete opposition to the revolutionary ideals and vision motivating change, thus teaching us bitter lessons.

In the midst of these many moral failures, the peoples' movements for non-violence inspired by Gandhi and Dr King shine like precious jewels of hope in human history. They demonstrate that, as you said, another way of life is possible – if we build another kind of world based on freedom and equality.

Gandhi believed that 'what is possible for one is possible for all'.[4] At first, the ideals of the non-violence movements were ridiculed as hopeless romanticism. Both the movements led by Gandhi and Dr King, however, achieved significant victories by courageously persevering with non-violent activism. They turned the impossible into the possible and changed the course of history. It is important to note that the essence of these movements was not simply the radical reform of social systems but the fundamental transformation of people's consciousness.

HARDING: There was a crucial recognition that the non-violent philosophy of Gandhi and King would have had no real meaning had they not lived it. Just as these two great men and their movements drew the attention of the entire world to non-violent acts of courage, it seems to me that we who live in a different age must continually confront the violence of our own era and work to combat it with new strategies effective in our times. Only by doing so will future generations understand and carry on the philosophy and emulate the examples King and Gandhi set with their lives.

IKEDA: The ones who will be most responsible for this mission of peace are the youth. They bring to this task a breath of fresh air, new perspectives and new ways of acting.

What perspectives do you feel are essential in the promotion of peace education?

Learning To Listen

HARDING: One of the most important aspects of peace education is learning how to listen. In my work with youth as well as adults, I encourage everyone to share the stories of their lives. I try to show that it is possible for people with different backgrounds, traditions and cultures to be open and share their stories with one another.

In working with youth, I have become convinced that they

often want to learn about people different from themselves. And so, sharing experiences and opinions is one of the main ways that I personally try to transmit the spirit and philosophy of non-violence. As I see it, at the heart of this spirit and philosophy is the determination to build an inclusive community that transcends artificial borders.

If young people can get to know people different from themselves, listen to their stories, work alongside them and begin to feel this same determination to build an inclusive community, then they have naturally learned about non-violence without even having discussed the topic. And they have learned what all spiritual masters teach, that our human differences are meant to draw us together in fascinating discovery, not to separate us in arrogance or fear.

IKEDA: Earlier in our dialogue, we touched upon the significance of stories (see Conversation Two), and stories in the context of peace education are certainly important. Every human being lives out a story that gives meaning to his or her existence – a story that depicts a precious, irreplaceable life history.

When we listen with an open heart to someone's story, we can learn from his or her rich store of experiences and wisdom conveyed in a narrative entirely different from our own. This can stimulate and expand our creative capacities, enabling us to weave new, vibrant stories of our own.

Dr King taught that people can learn even from those they perceive as enemies:

> Here is the true meaning and value of compassion and nonviolence, when they help us to see the enemy's point of view, to hear his questions, to know his assessment of ourselves. For from his view we may indeed see the basic weaknesses of our own condition, and if we are mature,

> we may learn and grow and profit from the wisdom of the brothers who are called the opposition.[5]

Our opponent is a human being, just like us. There is much that we can learn from our differences, new roads for us to discover. This concept in Dr King's philosophy expresses the fundamental spirit of dialogue and is inspiring and thought-provoking.

As I have been saying, Buddhism teaches that the Buddha nature resides in the life of every person. In order for people to transcend the boundaries of ally and opponent that separate them, a new story that depicts us all as human beings, all comrades dwelling together on this Earth, is needed.

HARDING: I am moved by how the humanitarian intellectual Hannah Arendt maintained that it is when we are in dialogue that we are most human. In this sense, peace education is about encouraging the best of our humanity, so that we eliminate our fears, our ignorance and our drive to dominate one another. Peace education reaches deep within our hearts and cultivates the strength to resist the efforts of nations and massive corporations to convince us by every means possible that war is necessary, that peace can be achieved through acts of mass destruction.

IKEDA: As you say, the goal of peace education is to bring out the best of our humanity – and it seems to me that this is the core of the movement that you and your colleagues have championed.

Gandhi summed up the solution in this way: 'If we are to reach real peace in this world . . . we shall have to begin with children.'[6] Indeed, peace begins with education. And education that fosters humanity is the foundation leading to peace. This means that the role of the educator is exceedingly important.

HARDING: In my peace education work with children and youth,

I have discovered that one of the key wishes that they continually express is that teachers listen to them. This taught me that the best peace educators are not those who can impart lots of knowledge and information to children but those who will nurture the practice of listening to them.

I would venture to guess that much of the strife and conflict that occurs in the world comes from people who, as children, never felt that they were heard. And so, as adults, they act out the anger and hurt resulting from their unfulfilled need to be recognized and listened to when they were children.

Consequently, peace-loving educators must constantly strive to understand how to nurture in children a sense that they are heard, loved, valued and full of great possibilities. This is transformative education.

IKEDA: To listen – to listen carefully to what the other person is saying – is the basic starting point for building a relationship with another person. It is essential.

Listening is a seemingly simple yet difficult act requiring patience and courage because we must have an underlying trust and respect for the other person. This is even more critical where children are concerned. It is important, as you say, for children to feel they are cared for, so that they will experience wholesome growth and development in their childhood.

A survey of Japanese elementary school students revealed how important it is to show children they are loved. The survey asked children what they wanted to hear most from their parents, and what they wanted to hear were the words 'You really did your best!' In second place was the comment 'You are smart. Good job!' And in third place were the words 'Thank you.'

According to the survey, children least wanted to hear their parents tell them, 'I knew you couldn't do it,' followed by 'You'll never be able to do it.' In third place was the admonition 'You need to study more.'

Children raised in an environment where they are affirmed and valued as individuals also affirm and respect others. This is the key to the flowering of a deep sense of humanity and to education for peace – not only for children but for adults. Dr King's non-violent struggle also started from this internal transformation.

Today's situation is naturally different than during Dr King's lifetime, but how do you think Dr King would have responded to the conflict and violence we currently see all around the globe?

HARDING: As I have mentioned, King was clear that to overcome conflict and confrontation we must stand up to three powerful social phenomena in American society. The first one that he mentioned was racism, which in the United States has been based on the beliefs of white supremacy. He urged us to see that this kind of viewpoint inevitably brings conflict.

Materialism was the second phenomenon to which King drew our attention. He felt that if we, as individuals or as nations, measure our worth solely by our material possessions, this puts us into direct conflict with others.

Militarism was the third phenomenon. He pointed out that we must resist the temptation to resort to militarism as the ultimate path to resolving conflicts on the local and national levels.

If King could see the widespread strife and conflict that we have in the world today, I am sure that he would continue his courageous actions, bringing the same kind of creativity that he poured into his struggles on behalf of the freedom movement in the 1950s and 1960s. If King were alive today, he would be in his eighties, and he would still be asking what role he could play or whom he could encourage to go help resolve a struggle going on somewhere. This is because he had the firm conviction that personal engagement was essential in bringing about a resolution to even the most difficult international conflicts.

IKEDA: This reminds me of the following passage in the Preamble of the UNESCO Constitution: 'Since wars begin in the minds of men, it is in the minds of men that the defences of peace must be constructed.'[7] Dr King's struggle was to overcome the malice and arrogance that dwell in people's hearts. The only way to do this is to begin by erecting a strong citadel of peace in each individual's heart, as hard as this may be.

According to Buddhist teachings, the three poisons of greed, anger and foolishness are at the root of all evil in human life. Nichiren wrote: 'In a country where the three poisons [of greed, anger, and foolishness] prevail to such a degree, how can there be peace and stability? . . . warfare occurs as a result of anger.'[8] The three poisons in people's lives lead to the calamities that befall a nation, he asserted. Warfare, he warned, occurs as a result of intensifying anger. He took action to spread the Buddhist philosophy of the dignity and worth of life to encourage a fundamental spiritual revolution and to help the people.

This is also the starting point of our Soka Gakkai International movement. It is the mission and responsibility of education and religion to show the sure way to peace.

How do you think we can nurture leaders for a new era who will advance the people's non-violence movement?

A Leadership Revolution

HARDING: When leaders are at their best, they are servants of the people. This perspective on leadership is closely linked to the spirit of the non-violence movement. In my view, training leaders must always be about nurturing a spirit of service.

IKEDA: We need to initiate a leadership revolution. Dr Rotblat said in one of our discussions that a requirement for the creation of global peace was to nurture a 'sense of loyalty to all of humanity' in people's hearts.[9] Together with such a global vision, leaders' actions must be based on the commitment to serve humanity.

In November 2010, I welcomed to Tokyo a party from the University of Massachusetts, Boston, led by Chancellor J. Keith Motley. In our discussions, he informed me with pride of the university's ideal of encouraging students to become leaders on the front line of public service.

Fostering leaders committed to serving the people, as you have indicated, is what we need to focus in the coming years.

How did Dr King endeavour to cultivate a successor?

HARDING: This question must be considered against the fact that King was only thirty-nine when he was assassinated. The question of leadership succession probably was not a priority for him.

Certainly, I don't think that the Southern Christian Leadership Conference placed much emphasis on preparing the next generation for leadership. Nevertheless, there were always many youth involved in SCLC campaigns. They were gaining experience from being part of the action. And King would always spend a lot of time with the younger people. He did not conduct any formal training, but wherever he went, he would ask to meet with young people in the local community.

Interestingly enough, he often sought out those young men who said they were in disagreement with him about the efficacy of non-violent struggle. Here again, he listened carefully to them and tried to open new ideas to them.

King led a life full of danger, and he was profoundly aware that his life could be taken at any time. That's probably one of the reasons he wanted to spend time with the young people.

IKEDA: Yes, that must have been his motivation in engaging with youth. It is such a tragedy that Dr King died at just thirty-nine, but he courageously gave his life for a noble cause. His life stands as an example to his youthful successors – a source of limitless courage and bright hope for future generations.

I know that Dr King was a precious comrade, but do you have teachers you have also looked up to throughout your life?

HARDING: The most important people for me were more like mentors. They were people whom I trusted and could talk to, and they taught me in informal ways.

One of my earliest mentors was the Reverend Phillip J. Bailey, the pastor of the little church where I grew up in Harlem. He was a magnificently self-educated man who studied hard and was knowledgeable about what was going on in the world. He saw his work as a pastor as an educational ministry.

Another mentor to me and teacher to many young people in the southern freedom movement was Ella Baker (see Conversation Five). She dedicated her life to the movement, and her life was a wonderful example for us all, especially in the development of what we now call 'participatory democracy'.

Finally, I must mention one more person, Howard Thurman, whom we discussed earlier (see Conversation Six).

IKEDA: When I met with Dr Lawrence E. Carter, dean of Morehouse College's Martin Luther King Jr International Chapel, we discussed Dr Thurman. Dean Carter emphasized that Morehouse College's greatest source of pride is counting Howard Thurman and Martin Luther King among its graduates.

'A dream is the bearer of a new possibility, the enlarged horizon, the great hope.'[10] These are famous words of Dr Thurman. His magnificent dream was a gift to the future of humanity.

I remember that when I met with you and Rosemarie, she spoke of the warm relationship your family had with the Thurman family. She strongly recommended that American women read Dr Thurman's *With Head and Heart: The Autobiography of Howard Thurman*. Rosemarie spoke highly of Dr Thurman's love for people – a love that encompassed the entire world and enabled him to overcome many difficulties and contribute to society.

HARDING: Howard Thurman's most important teaching was the fundamental message that we are all one. He emphasized that the universe is organized in a way that leads us to engage one another and unite to work for the common good and for the good of our communities.

Thurman was probably one of the first people who worked to develop a multiracial, inter-faith, religious congregation in our country. He did this in San Francisco at the end of World War II. Thurman knew that he was not the kind of leader who wanted to stand out in front and be recognized. He used to say that he would rather encourage the people going out on the front lines, help them find the resources they needed, and also be there for them when they came back. He wanted to help them to learn how to replenish the sources of strength and courage in their lives.

And he was an excellent listener. He would encourage people to see that they had great value. I believe that he was one of my greatest teachers.

IKEDA: Encountering a great teacher is one of life's most blessed gifts. With the passing of each year, I feel more and more grateful for the tutelage that I received from my mentor in my youth.

As we discussed before, when Dr Thurman spoke with Gandhi in India, he was inspired by Gandhi's philosophy of non-violence (see Conversation Six). When Thurman asked how individuals and communities could learn to employ the philosophy of *ahimsa* (non-violence), Gandhi answered:

> If for mastering of the physical sciences you have to devote a whole lifetime, how many lifetimes may be needed for mastering the greatest spiritual force that mankind has known? But why worry even if it means several lifetimes? For if this is the only permanent thing in life, if this is the only thing that counts, then whatever effort you bestow on mastering it is well spent.[11]

Even if we are unable to create a peaceful, non-violent global society in our generation, we must have faith that the next generation will strive to achieve it. If the next generation fails, then the generation after will surely step up to bring it into being.

I entrust my hope to the youth. The true spirit of peace education is found in unconditional faith in human beings and the unlimited potential of youth.

CONVERSATION FOURTEEN

Carrying the Legacy Forward

IKEDA: The true spirit of leadership is to focus on and act for the future, leaving a timeless spiritual treasure that illuminates the way forward.

Thank you for sharing an insightful outlook on the future at the forum 'This Noble Experiment: Developing the Democratic Spirit' at the Ikeda Centre for Peace, Learning, and Dialogue in November 2010. Your recollections of your many years of hard-fought battles for human rights inspired the audience and continue to have a far-reaching impact on the hearts and minds of many people. You asserted that, based on your own experiences, democracy is not a static governmental institution. Rather, it is a movement for finding freedom and self-reliance in the life of each person and establishing a path toward enlightened individual and social transformation.

You also observed that the noble path toward creating a true democracy had just begun, and that the goal will be reached through our patient, persistent efforts in dialogue with one another. If Dr King were alive today, I am sure that he would have agreed emphatically.

HARDING: I thoroughly enjoyed the opportunity to speak at the forum.

First of all, if King were still alive today, he would be in his eighties. He and I were close in age, so it is thought-provoking and fascinating to imagine what he would be like at eighty and older.[1] What would he be thinking? What actions would he be taking? Where would his heart and mind be taking him in this twenty-first-century world? These are thoughts that continually come to mind when I consider if King were alive today.

Come to think of it, President Ikeda, you are roughly the same age that King would have been today, and you were both born in January. Just as you do, King had an enormous sense of hope and possessed an insatiable inquiring mind, so I'm sure that you and he would have travelled similar paths.

King would have been in contact with all kinds of explorers – people exploring the spiritual realm, those pursuing intellectual inquiry, and those committed to transforming the world through social movements. All of these associations would have contributed to his continual growth and development.

IKEDA: Dr King said, 'Every crisis has both its dangers and opportunities. It can spell either salvation or doom.'[2] And Nichiren said: 'You should understand that, when one practices the Lotus Sutra under such circumstances, difficulties will arise, and these are to be looked on as "peaceful" practices',[3] and 'When great evil occurs, great good follows.'[4] Buddhism advocates living one's life based on the correct teaching, summoning all one's courage and wisdom, and turning adversity into opportunity, thus transforming one's circumstances.

While Dr King advanced the cause of human rights, he also addressed the problem of poverty, astutely observing, 'The agony of the poor impoverishes the wealthy; the betterment of the poor enriches the rich.'[5] The reality of our world, of course, is that there is a wide gap between the poor, the vast majority of the world's people, and the wealthy, a small minority. In many regions of the world, poverty is a source of conflict and civil war, a destabilizing force that threatens the entire social order.

HARDING: We can view poverty and conflict as existing in a dialectical relationship. For instance, the gap between the rich and poor widens as frequently occurring conflicts force more and more people into poverty and hunger. We can also see that poverty and hunger create conflict, and that conflict originates from economic disparity.

Indeed, this is another perspective on the three evils of racism, materialism and militarism that King identified, and which we have touched on before. These three evils continually reinforce one another in an evil system. They grow out of our inner thoughts, the mindsets that guide our actions.

If King were alive today, he would still be strongly urging us, through his words and deeds, to battle the mindset that gives birth to these three evils. He would surely be joining hands with others to explore and search for new ways to overcome the three evils, both in local communities and the international arena.

Each of us must re-examine our beliefs and change our values by engaging in a process of dialogue, both within ourselves and with others. In this way, we will surely reach the conclusion that, indeed, another, better world is possible. Therefore, encouraging dialogue, both inner and outer, is an important strategy to hasten the revolution of values that King so urgently called for.

By 'revolution of values', I do not mean simply reforming our values. Rather, I mean that we must undertake a complete conversion of our values on a more profound level.

LIMITED OR UNLIMITED?

IKEDA: Mahatma Gandhi appealed to our higher selves when he stated: 'Man's triumph will consist in substituting the struggle for existence by the struggle for mutual service. The law of the brute will be replaced by the law of man.'[6] This is the kind of conversion of core values that Dr King called for so emphatically.

More than a century ago, at a time when Japan was lurching dangerously toward militarism, Tsunesaburo Makiguchi urged humankind to transition away from competition in the military, political and economic spheres. He envisioned a new stage in which people and nations vie for the most humanitarian ways of living and governing. Focusing solely on military, economic and political prowess encourages self-interest and conflict, and gives priority to the principle that might makes right. President Makiguchi saw that the world needed 'humanitarian competition', in which people strive to cooperate and build a society of peaceful coexistence.

Mr Makiguchi explained his concept in this way:

> The important thing is the setting of a goal of well being and protection of all people, including oneself but not at the increase of self interest alone. In other words, the aim is the betterment of others and in doing so, one chooses ways that will yield personal benefit as well as benefit to others.[7]

His vision of humanitarian competition was characterized by mutual respect, mutual assistance, mutual encouragement, mutual inspiration and mutual growth.

Dr King also voiced his concern about competition when he wrote:

> Somehow we must transform the dynamics of the world power struggle from the nuclear arms race, which no one can win, to a creative contest to harness man's genius for the purpose of making peace and prosperity a reality for all

> the nations of the world. In short, we must shift the arms race into a 'peace race'.[8]

These concepts of a peace race and humanitarian competition appeared in different eras, under different conditions, but they are in harmony.

HARDING: Personally, the approach I would take is not to develop humanitarian competition, or competition for goodness, but to talk in terms of supporting mutual encouragement, ways that we can encourage one another more. I am more comfortable with this perspective – the idea that encouraging one another is most important.

In any case, I would choose to help people to draw from a deep place within themselves the resources to develop their capacity to serve and encourage others. The urgency of the times demands that we turn from the madness of military and economic competition to the more sane and sober relationships of human cooperation.

IKEDA: You mention the idea of people developing their latent capacity to serve and encourage others. Indeed, it is increasingly important for us to discover how to draw out this latent capacity and utilize it for the benefit of society.

This was a major issue that arose in a dialogue I conducted with Dr Aurelio Peccei.[9] The Club of Rome, which Dr Peccei founded, is famous for sounding the alarm with its 1972 report *Limits to Growth*. 'Limits to growth' refers to the limits of the Earth's declining resources, the danger of exceeding the limited capacity of the Earth to recover from environmental pollution, and also the limits of the Earth and its finite resources to satisfy human greed.

But there are no limits to the growth of human capacity to serve others. One of the conclusions of our dialogue was that we must recognize and develop this enormous, latent potential.

HARDING: This reminds me of a book called *Gandhi the Man*. The introduction mentions a BBC documentary, *Gandhi's India*, based on several interviews with people who had worked with Gandhi. The interviewer asked one woman, Asha Devi, who had been close to Gandhi, 'Don't you think that he was a bit unrealistic, that he failed to reckon with the limits of our capacities?' She responded with a twinkle in her eyes, 'There are no limits to our capacities.'[10]

When we think about athletes engaged in serious physical training, they discover capacities, as I understand it, that they never imagined that they had. The assumption they begin with is that they will surpass their present capacity by committing themselves to continuous training.

Perhaps this understanding can be applied to human development – the development of our ability to serve one another and help one another to grow and develop. Even though we have unlimited potential, we assume that we are limited. Through this mistaken assumption, we impose limits on the development of our potential. As Gandhi taught, there are great discoveries yet to be made in the realm of non-violence that will surpass every conceivable kind of weapon of violence that we have ever created.

We Are Them, They Are Us

IKEDA: We must open our eyes to the infinite potential that every person possesses. Religion's mission, in the broadest sense, is to conquer the ego and motivate us to serve and encourage one another.

The social practice of the bodhisattva way of Mahayana Buddhism, based on the philosophy of the sanctity of life, is to boldly, courageously strive in our daily lives to overcome self-interest, contribute to others and to society, live a good life and elevate ourselves.

The way of the bodhisattva shows that it is impossible to

overcome our internal evils without engaging in a courageous struggle against external evils. Dr King also pointed out the inverse – that we must battle our internal evils if we are to triumph over external evils.

HARDING: Here again, we must think in dialectical terms. It would be dangerous to mechanistically try to *first* complete our inner work and *then* deal with our outer work. This is because both are mutually supportive parts of a whole, a larger entity.

For example, while we are in the midst of struggling to overcome our internal evils, if we turn our attention to the external evils, we may discover perspectives that help with our internal struggles. Conversely, our battle against our internal evils may provide valuable insights into ways to tackle the external evils.

King and Gandhi and others encouraged us to understand that our perception of the 'enemy' is a projection of the struggles occurring in our interior selves. They wanted to convey the insight that the enemy, whom we view as 'them', is connected to us more intimately than we think. That is to say, on a profound level, we are all the same. We are 'them', and they are us, and this realization can only help transform the way we engage with 'them' in our struggles.

IKEDA: The non-violent struggle is a struggle against such external evils as discrimination and oppression, and at the same time a struggle against the fundamental inner evils of hatred and greed. The true significance of the human rights struggles waged by you, Dr King, and others lies not simply in reforming laws and systems but in building a humane society in which people can live fully human lives. Indeed, its significance is in striving for a society of peaceful coexistence that transcends the fractious issues of race and ideology, a society in which the dignity of each person shines brilliantly.

HARDING: It is interesting to note that there was a major difference between the American and the Indian non-violence movements. The difference lies in the reality that in the United States, the citizens pushing for social change had to, ultimately, coexist with the very people who had put up the walls of prejudice that had kept them from participating in civic life.

In his book *Where Do We Go From Here: Chaos or Community?*, which I am currently re-reading, King discussed this fact. He explained that many of the people who responded to the freedom movement by creating civil rights laws were not actually motivated by a desire to build an egalitarian society. Consequently, we are still fighting many of the same battles today.

IKEDA: The abolition of a discriminatory system does not mean that the hearts of those who perpetrated the discrimination will be touched and transformed. This is why it is imperative to change the urge in people's hearts and minds to discriminate and dominate. Dr King continued to struggle till the end, not simply to reform the system but to tackle this much more intractable problem.

HARDING: Therefore, we must not only struggle to conquer evil but must commit our efforts to create goodness and virtue. We must push ahead to battle on both the internal and external fronts.

For example, in order to triumph over our internal evils, it is essential that we cultivate a vision of a new society. Moreover, as you know, my brother, this battle against internal evil is waged not only through meditation or chanting the sutras. We are seeking to create a new social order, a new concept of community. This will simultaneously contribute to building a new internal order – a new mindset within ourselves and among ourselves. Again, King liked to say, 'We've got to organize goodness.'

IKEDA: The true purpose of religion is not to observe formalities or rituals. It is to give people the strength to live the best life possible and to infuse society with a dynamic, vibrant spirituality and philosophy of life.

This reminds me of an anecdote about Gandhi. One day, he came across a Brahman who kept insisting that Gandhi forsake the mundane world of social and political movements and choose the cloistered existence of meditation. Gandhi replied that while his days were in fact devoted to efforts to attain the spiritual liberation of enlightenment, he felt no need to withdraw to a cave for that purpose. The cave, he said, was something that he carried within him.

Gandhi's everyday struggles were, for him, a form of religious practice and a path to the liberation of his soul. Religion in Gandhi's understanding was simultaneously the source of inspiration for all the activities of human life and the means by which we can realize a humane, just society in which every person can thrive. Gandhi also believed that religion should manifest a spirit of non-violence and genuine humanism, based on truth, within our current political and social reality.

Women Achieving Their Full Potential

Ikeda: When we contemplate the creation of this kind of humane, peaceful and non-violent society, we must never forget the indispensable role that women can play. Women have a wonderful, dynamic power to influence people's hearts.

You have recognized and praised the role that women have played in human rights movements. Can you share more examples of women who have inspired you?

Harding: Several women come to mind, including some active over a long period. One woman who is one of the wisest I've known in the field of social change is Grace Lee Boggs. Born in 1915, she has been involved in movements for social change for more than six decades as an activist and political thinker.

Another woman who has made an enormous contribution over many years is Dolores Huerta. She and her co-worker, Cesar Chavez, co-founded the United Farm Workers Union. Now in her eighties, Dolores is still working for social change and viewing the world through humanistic eyes.

The poet Sonia Sanchez is still another heaven-sent gift to us all. She continues to fight for as well as compose poetry for social change. In this same way, Alice Walker, a poet, essayist and novelist, is someone whom I value highly for her vision of what is possible and her willingness to act on her convictions. Just recently, I called her house, and she was out, but I was struck by her answering machine message. At the end of the message, after all these instructions to various people, her message to everyone who called was 'I love you. I really love you. Just hold on to that.' As you may know, Alice Walker has been a powerful champion of human rights of all kinds, as evidenced by her great love for the Earth itself, for the life of the planet; her deep concern about the injustices suffered by the Palestinian people; and her determination that justice and equality be available to people of all sexual orientations.

IKEDA: You have introduced us to extraordinary people. What would you say are the common characteristics of these women, whom you hold in such high regard and with whom you share a similar vision?

HARDING: Perhaps one characteristic that they all share is a profound sense of appreciation for their ancestors and their roots. They understand that their strength and ability to reach out to others is drawn from their cultural and ancestral roots.

A related characteristic is the capacity of these women to combine love and the struggle, in the sense that they are motivated by deep love to fight for the common good. By their example, they remind us that love and struggle are not contradictory elements in the hearts and minds of those who engage in social activism.

IKEDA: Women indeed possess in abundance an excellent capacity to convert conflict into harmony and division into unity. Gandhi, not surprisingly, honoured and appreciated this aptitude in women and held high expectations for them. In fact, women stood beside and fought bravely with Gandhi on the front lines of the movement for the non-violent liberation of India.

Nichiren also recognized women and their contributions to the Buddhist cause of honouring the sanctity of life, praising them highly and encouraging them in their activities. In an age in which the status of women was low, Nichiren declared, 'There should be no discrimination among those who propagate the five characters of Myoho-renge-kyo in the Latter Day of the Law, be they men or women.'[11] He also praised the depth of women's spirituality: 'A woman who embraces this [Lotus] sutra not only excels all other women, but also surpasses all men.'[12]

Can you tell me more about some of the women who worked with Dr King in the civil rights movement?

HARDING: There were many powerful women who worked closely with King. One of them whom I have mentioned before was Ella Jo Baker (see Conversation Five and Conversation Eight). Others were Septima Clark and Dorothy Cotton, who worked with King in the area of citizenship education. King appreciated all of their contributions. He was blessed to have worked with so many exceptionally talented women in the freedom movement. Of course, influenced as he was by the patriarchal tendencies of the black church tradition, King often had to fight his way through to the fullest appreciation of such women co-workers.

Another woman especially important to me was Fannie Lou Hamer. She was a significant grassroots participant in the movement. Though she had little formal education – not unlike many of the participants in the movement – she was a woman of great wisdom, great intelligence and great courage. And she had a keen musical talent that helped uplift and unify the hearts and spirits of all who participated in the campaigns. She also had a wonderful sense of humour and a strong belief in the movement.

As I have mentioned many times, the freedom movement did not depend on the leadership of one charismatic leader; it was a grassroots movement arising from community organizing all over the South. Consequently, it is important to recognize that women made up the heart of the movement, just as they occupied the heart of their communities.

Basically, if women had not encouraged and organized people to attend the mass meetings, no one would have come to hear the leaders, and the meeting halls would have been empty. If women had not encouraged and inspired people to participate in the marches, there would have been no one to march. This also applies to the Montgomery bus boycott, that central story of our movement.

Well before the bus boycott, many women had been active in discussing and thinking about the issue of segregation and the humiliation it was causing in Montgomery, especially in the transportation system. They were known as the Women's Political Council and were led by Jo Ann Gibson Robinson, a local college professor. When Rosa Parks was arrested that historic evening for refusing to sit at the back of the bus, Jo Ann heard about it and took action.

She took it upon herself to go to the segregated college where she taught to mimeograph more than 35,000 copies of a flier calling people to a mass meeting in response to Parks's arrest. She did this all by herself on one of those old mimeograph machines, the predecessor of today's photocopy machine – a task much more time- and energy-consuming than it would be today. Her work literally led to the first mass meeting called to support Rosa Parks and develop a boycott of the buses.

Thousands of people came to that meeting. This was a testament to the community-organizing power of women. Women like this throughout the movement inspired people, strengthened them and guided them to participate.

Of course, as I have mentioned before, Rosemarie, my dear wife, was one of the great women spirits of the movement. She epitomized deep wisdom, gentle love and fierce, courageous determination.

IKEDA: Rosemarie was a great woman and your beloved comrade in arms.

The Soka Gakkai could be called 'the Soka Women's Gakkai' because it is supported by the power of many hardworking women. The power of women has been decisive in advancing the organization's grassroots movement for peace and culture. The majority of these women are unsung heroes. Awakened to their noble mission through the pursuit of their human revolution, they have created a mighty people's movement by encouraging people, rallying them, inspiring them and rousing them to action.

The sense of solidarity and fellowship they have created has spread throughout the world to 192 countries and territories. There has never been a movement of this kind in Buddhist history. Through their courageous faith as individuals, they have achieved a great transformation, liberating themselves from the shackles of their personal karma and, while growing as people, joining with others in a network for building peace.

How can we encourage, cherish and support these extraordinary women to realize their power? It is certainly no exaggeration to say that the future prospects of the Soka Gakkai International depend on how well we meet this goal.

HARDING: One of the tasks of any great movement is to encourage women to achieve their full potential. It is important to work with women as they realize their God-given gifts and free themselves from the internal bonds that limit their growth, as well as from the external bonds that we men often create.

It is also important to urge men to open their eyes. We must see and respect women as a resource of untapped leadership potential.

IKEDA: Exactly. Gandhi advocated for an enlightened view of women: 'If by strength is meant moral power, then woman is immeasurably man's superior.'[13] He also felt that 'if non-violence is the law of our being, the future is with woman'.[14]

In the twenty-first century, a civilization that respects the sanctity of life will be built only when people, and especially women, bring their profound, latent potential into full play.

CONVERSATION FIFTEEN

Start With a Dream

IKEDA: Walt Whitman, extolling the ideals of democracy, said:

> America should now stand for the world – should bear witness not only to her own success, but human solidarity, universal union, the largest possible circles of comradeship.[1]

I sense that the grand dream cherished by Whitman and the great dream espoused by Dr King for the harmonious coexistence of humankind share a profound, timeless affinity.

Speaking of the word *dream*, the familiar expression 'the American dream' reflects new opportunities and the possibility of a better life. It is said that the American historian James Truslow Adams coined this expression, though it has come to mean different things to different people.

What are your thoughts on 'the American dream'?

HARDING: The nineteenth- and twentieth-century perception of America for many people was of a country of enormous material wealth. The expression 'the American dream' tended to elicit a materialistic interpretation.

However, Langston Hughes, who wrote many poems about his dream of America, passionately expressed his belief in the ideals of freedom, justice and equality. Martin Luther King, who lived the American struggle for black liberation, also emphasized these ideals. King called on us to envision America as a place of human and spiritual wealth, a place where people can manifest their highest potential. This was the heart of his dream, very close to Whitman's.

IKEDA: Dr King reminded people of the high ideals on which America was founded. He devoted his entire life to sharing his dream. In his 'I Have a Dream' speech during the March on Washington, he made the following appeal:

> So I say to you, my friends, that even though we must face the difficulties of today and tomorrow, I still have a dream. It is a dream deeply rooted in the American dream that one day this nation will rise up and live out the true meaning of its creed – we hold these truths to be self-evident, that all men are created equal.[2]

Dr King was yearning for the day when America would fulfil the promise of its founding ideals enshrined in the Declaration of Independence.

HARDING: Also, the Preamble to our Constitution contains the idea that we Americans are obligated to carry on the work of creating a 'more perfect Union', a more perfect democracy. King and the movement struggled to give substance to this ideal, this dream.

The magnificent concept of the American dream is a country that is the best that it can be. In this sense, material prosperity is just a small part of the dream. King's contribution was to transform and deepen our understanding of the American dream.

All the poets who have reflected on this, from Walt Whitman to

Langston Hughes, have encouraged us to dream about the possibilities for a better world. They did not know how those dreams could become reality or be integrated into everyday life, but we can be sure that nothing is possible unless we dream it first. While we will not stop at the dreaming stage, we cannot start anything without dreaming.

IKEDA: Great dreams nurture extraordinary people, inspire great struggles and build great lives, leading ultimately to a new, brighter future. My wish for young people, who bear the responsibility for creating the future, is that they pursue their dreams with courage and conviction. This is the message that I have consistently emphasized over the years.

I recall that my mentor would often say:

> It's perfectly all right for youth to cherish dreams that may seem almost too big. What we can achieve in a single lifetime is always but a fraction of what we would like to achieve. So if you start out with expectations that are too low, you'll end up not accomplishing anything at all.[3]

My dream has been to help bring into being the noble vision of my mentor. After World War II, Mr Toda undertook a people's movement for peace based on Buddhism. As his disciple, I took to heart my mentor's wish and tirelessly travelled the globe for decades to help realize his vision.

Our focus now should be on the youth who will live into the future. We should inspire them and endow them with hope, courage and a vision enabling them to live out their dreams. The role of education is especially important in this respect.

DEMOCRATIC CITIZENSHIP

HARDING: The other day, someone told me about a public school competition that was held in the Midwest in which students wrote letters to President Obama, telling him what they wanted him to do to create a better America. We need to devise more ways to encourage young people to think about what it means to create a better world and to challenge them to imagine what their role might be in developing this world.

During the past approximately twenty years, a question that has always been foremost in my mind has been what kind of education is essential in preparing people for democratic citizenship. Just because we have been born in America does not automatically mean that we understand the possibilities and power that can be manifested by a democratic America.

A baby born of a human mother does not immediately understand the significance of being human. Likewise, a sense of democratic citizenship is something that must be nurtured in people.

Accordingly, a major task that will shape the next period of American history is to develop an effective and inspiring educational process that nurtures democratic citizens. This task must include building the kind of foundation that we see in all the great religious traditions of the world. Most important is to realize that we have the capacity within us to become far more perfected human beings than we are now.

IKEDA: This is a point that you have emphasized consistently – that the solidarity of enlightened citizens who understand and embody the democratic spirit is essential for the development of a healthy democracy.

Whitman called democracy the dream of a new land and asserted that it provided a 'training school' and 'life's gymnasium' for producing first-class citizens. He emphasized spiritual values in saying that to fulfil its role, democracy needed to produce copious numbers of such citizens through the 'advent of a sane and pervading religiousness'.[4]

The concept of equality is the essence of Mahayana Buddhism. Buddhism recognizes a sacred potential – the Buddha nature – in every human being and offers a concrete path for making the worth and dignity of the individual and all life shine their brightest. The only way to build a vital society is to foster this spirit of equality in the heart of each individual. As you have said, the first important step is to tirelessly encourage people to awaken to their extraordinary potential.

HARDING: Consider Whitman's 'life's gymnasium': Perhaps this is where we can exercise and practise to bring out our best gifts. Here again, I am reminded of the words of Langston Hughes – he wrote a wonderful poem called 'Let America Be America Again'.

For many of us – especially women, Native Americans, African Americans, other people of colour and, most of all, poor people – America has never lived up to its ideals, and we are completely justified in making Langston's claim that 'America never was America to me.' But he didn't stop at that complaint. He continued, 'And yet I swear this oath – America will be!'[5]

IKEDA: He affirmed a commitment and challenging spirit to realize the highest ideals: 'Let America be America again. / Let it be the dream it used to be.'[6] The promise of American democracy – this beacon of hope that is the American dream in its purest sense, which has still not been achieved – burned brightly in Langston Hughes's heart.

In another poem, Hughes wrote, 'We have tomorrow / Bright before us / Like a flame.'[7] He raises a noble image of the American people that I find immensely appealing – hardy and powerful as they continue their advance toward a more hopeful tomorrow.

HARDING: The task of building a better America – the best possible America – is one that requires the participation of every person. We should not wait for presidents or legislators to lead the way. Rather, each of us must nurture ourselves and one another so that we can work individually and together to fulfil the American dream of a 'more perfect Union'.

Transformation in a democratic society does not begin with a strong, charismatic leader. Rather, it begins with the fierce determination of the people to transform their reality. Only when the aspirations of the people well up in a mighty surge will the times begin to change for the better. This was certainly our experience in the southern freedom movement after World War II.

IKEDA: The people are the central actors in an era's reformation, and the human revolution within each person is the driving force for a new era's creation.

In my youth, my mentor told me: 'That which we resolve to undertake is a bloodless revolution, one which does not victimize even a single person. It is an unduplicated revolution.'[8] The Soka Gakkai has championed a revolution of the people, by the people, and for the people, based on the Buddhist philosophy of the sanctity of life. The Soka Gakkai does not have any clergy enjoying special status. Each person is a central player and fulfils a key role in the movement.

How do we bring people together, motivate them and tap their initiative and self-motivation? This is the mission and significance of the Soka Gakkai International in every region of the world. Learning from our predecessors' challenges and achievements, and collaborating and cooperating with many other citizens' movements, we hope to further expand our movement.

Education for Change

HARDING: In educational programmes designed to cultivate citizens who embody the spirit of democracy, it is essential to teach the stories of those who have dedicated themselves to the struggle to form a 'more perfect Union'. One of the best examples to include in this education is the story of the movement to abolish slavery. Every child should know about this powerful struggle and the deep sacrifices that Americans, both black and white, made to erase the stain of slavery from the life of the nation.

Once, I was speaking to a group of schoolchildren about stories of the movement. I showed some film clips from the documentary *Eyes on the Prize*. One showed the iconic images of King and his associates marching from Selma to Montgomery and, after overcoming much pain and hardship, finally crossing over the Alabama River on the Pettus Bridge. This was the march they attempted after the 7 March 1965, Bloody Sunday incident.[9]

As we watched the clip, I called the children's attention to a striking white-haired man with a long white beard marching close to King. I told them that his name was Abraham J. Heschel, a great Jewish rabbi, and I asked them if they could imagine themselves participating in this march, too. One little boy, perhaps six or seven, kept waving his hands while others were speaking.

When I finally called on him, he said: 'I was there. I was there.'

I said, 'Really?'

And he answered: 'Yes. My name is Abraham, too.'

It was a moment that I will never forget. Children are ready and waiting to be called upon to join the struggle.

IKEDA: It's important to teach children the meaning and importance of human rights from an early age in an understandable way.

In my 2011 peace proposal,[10] which emphasized the importance of the culture of human rights, I made several recommendations, including the establishment of a specialized UN agency to promote human rights education. I referred to your words on the importance of passing the human rights struggle on to succeeding generations and continually expanding democracy.[11] One of the most important tasks of humanistic education is to pass on the spirit and legacy of former generations' struggles to the young people, the future leaders of society.

Rabbi Heschel was one of the most important Jewish philosophers of the twentieth century. He went to America to escape Nazi persecution and participated in the freedom movement and the anti-Vietnam War movement. As one who had experienced the evils of racial discrimination, he joined Dr King and the freedom movement and was highly critical of any kind of racial discrimination. He asserted:

> Few of us realize that racism is man's gravest threat to man, the maximum of hatred for a minimum of reason, the maximum of cruelty for a minimum of thinking.[12]

Regrettably, even now in the twenty-first century, these stupid, senseless acts of discrimination still continue in many places around the world, causing countless individuals hardship and suffering. Since the dawn of recorded history, we know that humans have devoted themselves to endless technological progress. However, human consciousness does not have a corresponding maturity. In the twentieth century, in which each ensuing war used more advanced technological weaponry, unprecedented numbers of lives were lost.

This reminds us that science and knowledge alone will never rid society of suffering. In this sense, the advancement of science and technology force us to question the kind of education we need to perfect and elevate ourselves as human beings.

HARDING: I recognize that science and technology must be an essential part of a twenty-first-century education. However, they should be given second or third place in priority.

Do we even understand what science and technology are for?

We never will if we fail to acknowledge the capacities of the human spirit and to envision positive social change.

Unless science and technology are employed in the work of creating a more just, democratic and benevolent society, we could easily find ourselves in the same situation as Hitler's Germany. At that point in the twentieth century, Germany possessed the most advanced science and technology in the world. This tells us that science and technology must be grounded in something deeper, something that has a more meaningful purpose – or else they are absolutely dangerous and threaten the very existence of humanity.

IKEDA: Nothing is more frightening than the reckless advance of science governed by a misguided philosophy and objectives that threaten the sanctity of human life. We indeed must ask, 'What is the true purpose of science?' The answer must always be that it is for the sake of humanity's welfare. The more science and technology develop, the more urgently we need a philosophy to control and direct their application to human happiness, the more we need an enlightened ethical perspective and an educational system and social environment that concretely actualize this perspective.

Not long after World War II, in 1949, my mentor insisted:

> A true religion must guide science to serve the interests of peace and the happiness of humanity, and it must ensure that science creates the conditions for the happiness and welfare of all people.

This depends, in the end, on how well each of us as individuals can perfect and elevate our qualities as human beings.

Former South African president Nelson Mandela, whom I admire and respect, said, 'One of the most difficult things is not to change society – but to change yourself.'[13] A major task for education is to cultivate this ability.

HARDING: Education that seeks to cultivate agents of change must focus on helping people examine their external as well as their internal worlds. People must come to know themselves and their internal development processes in order to understand how others developed their spirits and achieved what they did.

As a historian, I focus on the facts that reveal who advocated for change and who did not want to see change take place. And I want to know why those people resisted change. In determining the answer, I want to understand not only the historical reasons but also the internal issues that made people act the way they did.

We must understand the immense forces within us that inspire us to work for social change as well as the internal obstacles that make us resist this drive. It is the purview of education to explore the theme of how people overcame the resistance arising from their internal obstacles.

BEST BRIDGE WE HAVE

IKEDA: This is an important exploration – one that reveals the essence of human nature and society. I understand well that the human rights struggle you have championed is also a spiritual quest in which people seek truth and inner transformation as they strive to establish a society free from discrimination. This is precisely the area on which contemporary education should focus.

At this point, I want to affirm the importance of promoting the arts and a poetic sensibility in education. Humanistic education must foster artistic and poetic sensibilities, which train and cultivate the human spirit, along with knowledge, reasoning powers and a firm moral foundation.

Whitman wrote, 'Nothing is plainer than the need, a long period to come, of a fusion of the States into the only reliable identity, the moral and artistic one.'[14] Regarding the significance and importance of poetry, Whitman wrote, 'Like her [America], it [poetry] must place in the van, and hold up at all hazards, the banner of the divine pride of man in himself, (the radical foundation of the new religion).'[15]

John Dewey, one of the most influential American philosophers of education, placed particular emphasis on the role of the arts in education. The arts and poetry are expressions of the vibrancy of human life and thus have the power to foster empathy and bring people together.

HARDING: Any educational programme to enhance human development and cultivate a sense of humanity should always include the arts. In the revised edition of my book *Hope and History*, I created a new chapter specifically focusing on the role of the artist in the development of a democratic society. The arts should be at the heart of an education that helps us to become more human.

Poetry, especially, gives us some creative ways to think about the story of our lives. This is because poets are constantly trying to reach into the depths of our reality.

When King spoke about his dream, it was important that he mentioned the work of Langston Hughes, who stimulates us to think about what a dream really is. He takes the experience that King is speaking about and expresses it in a different way and with different language.

Hughes wrote many poems about dreams. In one titled 'Dreams', he wrote, 'Hold fast to dreams / For if dreams die / Life is a broken-winged bird / That cannot fly.'[16]

Poetry can remind us that we have the capacity to create – the capacity of telling and understanding our stories. But its role does not stop there. It stimulates us to take on the task of imagining a new future – an essentially poetic task.

It may be that we should not try to describe the future simply in ordinary prose, scientific paragraphs or straight statements of proof. Maybe we should express it in poetry because this may be the best bridge we have between that which exists and that which is yet to come.

IKEDA: To reclaim the American dream in this new century, we must indeed restore in our hearts a powerful poetic sensibility.

Thank you for presenting me with the revised edition of *Hope and History*, which I immediately introduced to our readers in the *Seikyo Shimbun*. I found it significant that you emphasized the important role of the arts in effecting social change.

The struggle that you and Dr King engaged in to realize the American dream seems to me to have been an actualization of the founding fathers' poetic vision – the nation's founding principles. It is a struggle that goes on to this day.

HARDING: I don't believe that America or its leadership ever held firm to those founding ideas. As Thurgood Marshall, the first African-American Supreme Court Justice, said so frankly, we have to realize that those slaveholders and slave traders at the heart of this country's founding did not know what they were talking about when they spoke of democracy and justice for all.

The institution of slavery is a wound that existed at the time of the founding of the country, and each step we take must be toward healing that wound. That's why we, and every generation that follows, must envision the kind of free, multiracial and democratic American society that we want today and repeatedly try to build that society until we get it right.

IKEDA: And at that time, the American dream envisioned by Dr King will shine brightly in each individual's heart.

It is easy to become discouraged by the hardships of our reality and to become cynical and even give up the struggle. However, only by daring to take on life's challenges can we develop ourselves and achieve spiritual victory.

We can always hold on to our dreams, and, indeed, we must. But why? Because we possess in our hearts the enormous courage and hope enabling us to overcome all suffering and hardship. Within each of us is an indefatigable life force.

This dynamic wellspring of life is the source of the American dream. Many formidable obstacles and hostile reactions must be overcome to fulfil this dream. Dr King, however, urged us to develop the quality of always looking for the silver lining, any negatives notwithstanding.

Even in the face of adversity, we want to keep moving forward with a strong fighting spirit. No matter what happens, we want to continue to advance our struggle, with hope and cheer in our hearts. We believe that at the conclusion of our steadfast struggle, humanity's dream will surely embrace us in its brilliant radiance.

CONVERSATION SIXTEEN

Becoming World Citizens

IKEDA: As we bring our dialogue to a close, let's address the tide of globalization that is sweeping the world today. Even in his time, Dr King had a keen sense of this impending wave of globalization. In a speech delivered on 31 March 1968, just four days before his assassination, Dr King told his audience: 'We are challenged to develop a world perspective. No individual can live alone, no nation can live alone, and anyone who feels that he can live alone is sleeping through a revolution.'[1]

Dr King already knew instinctively that humanity shares a common destiny, and that we must choose a path that seeks peaceful coexistence and mutual prosperity for all. He had a powerful sense that humanity must throw off the shackles of hatred and greed, and put a stop to the recurring conflicts and violence.

HARDING: Globalization is a process that bears the marks of human intention, unlike natural phenomena such as the monsoons that sweep across Southeast Asia. It is made possible by economic, political and cultural structures driven by human desire.

For many, globalization is a source of new wealth and power.

However, for the vast majority, it is a source of continuing distress and deeper poverty. This is why we must discern what we can do to make the forces of globalization serve humankind.

IKEDA: Dr King's words remain relevant to this day. He continued with this observation: 'Through our scientific and technological genius, we have made of this world a neighbourhood and yet we have not had the ethical commitment to make of it a brotherhood.'[2]

Every thoughtful individual must be painfully aware of this fact. Again, our progress in human consciousness lags far behind our advances in science and technology. This was one of the conclusions that emerged from my dialogue with Arnold Toynbee. Dr Toynbee declared that human dignity, which is so essential to human happiness, could be achieved only in the field of ethics: 'The disparity between our technology and our ethics is greater today than it has ever been.'[3] While seeking to create a prosperous society, we must seek even more to build a humane society that allows people to live fully human lives.

HARDING: I want to, first of all, point out that if King were alive today, he probably would have moved away from using the term *brotherhood* to express the idea of human community. By this, I mean that *brotherhood* reflects a traditional, male-dominant perspective. Therefore, it would be entirely appropriate for us to rephrase his idea as he would want to express it today. I think he would say, 'Although we've made the world a neighborhood, we have failed to make it a loving community through moral commitment.'

How, then, should we go about building this 'loving community'? A major contribution to this task is sharing 'good news' – making widely available examples of individuals and groups engaged in building loving communities. This is information unknown to most people.

I have thought for a long time that some media practitioners should develop a 'good news' network. It would be a network that identifies and broadcasts positive, encouraging news emerging from local communities as well as the global community.

IKEDA: Media that offers 'good news' – even if about the small events of daily life – and thus inspires people can be a source of strength and hope.

In this age of globalization and information technology, media is currently undergoing a radical transformation and diversification. Through the Internet, new knowledge and information are with each passing moment broadcast and shared with people everywhere. The public's attention inevitably tends to be drawn to the most sensational news and events. That is precisely why, to stimulate positive social change and development, we need to make a steadfast commitment to transmitting 'good news' that, focusing primarily on local endeavours, draws people closer together.

After World War II, when our organization was evolving into a grassroots movement for peace, culture and education, my mentor saw that we were entering an age of mass media, and we began to talk about founding a newspaper. In the beginning, the newspaper was published three times a month. It was a somewhat homegrown publication, created primarily by Mr Toda and me.

Mr Toda used to say that he wanted people all over Japan and the world to read the *Seikyo Shimbun*, so at the beginning of our fifth year of publication, we began to send complimentary copies to ten Asian leaders, including Jawaharlal Nehru, prime minister of India; Ramon Magsaysay, president of the Philippines; Mao Zedong, chairman of the People's Republic of China; and Zhou Enlai, China's premier.

At that time, the Soka Gakkai was still a small organization, and some ridiculed our audacity. Nevertheless, I was determined to carry on the wish of my mentor, and we have continued to this day to make every effort to improve the paper, to make it one that offers hope and courage to ordinary people.

The expansion of our movement to protect freedom of religion, promote dialogue, and create a century of peace and humanity has unfolded in tandem with the *Seikyo Shimbun*'s growth and development, so I am aware of how important it is to disseminate inspiring information.

Also, I am convinced that a highly literate populace and a positive reading culture are critical. Consequently, we are focusing our efforts in this area.

HARDING: The Internet can have a positive or negative influence on the path of globalization. In many places around the world, it seems to me that the Internet is being used creatively as a way of sharing information about non-violent practices, such as in the essentially youth-led revolutions in Egypt, Tunisia and elsewhere in the Arab Spring. It is clear that this new means of communication is enabling people to share their hope that another world is indeed possible.

The goal of our work in the Veterans of Hope Project is to unite young people by transcending every kind of boundary, whether it be social, political, racial or economic. What if this goal could be achieved in a multicultural and multinational educational setting? Students would have the opportunity to deepen their understanding not only of their own values but also of the values of people in completely different circumstances from themselves.

IKEDA: By encouraging interaction and exchange among youth raised in many different cultures, new ways of thinking will evolve that will surely create a new sense of solidarity and unity. As they come to understand one another, learn from one another and contribute to one another's growth and development, they will succeed in building a new era. I am sure that, as a result, when they meet a new person, they will, first of all, sense the simple fact that the other person is a human being just like themselves – this before they become aware of the differences, such as those of culture, religion or race.

In the speech I mentioned earlier, Dr King also said:

> For some strange reason I can never be what I ought to be until you are what you ought to be. And you can never be what you ought to be until I am what I ought to be. This is the way God's universe is made; this is the way it is structured.[4]

At this point in his speech, Dr King quoted these famous words from the English poet John Donne:

> No man is an island entire of itself. Every man is a piece of the continent, a part of the main . . . Any man's death diminishes me because I am involved in mankind; therefore never send to know for whom the bell tolls; it tolls for thee.[5]

Donne's insight resonates with the Buddhist view of dependent origination: All human beings are connected to one another. Thus, encouraging another person through dialogue also serves to encourage yourself. Likewise, to awaken another is to awaken yourself. To pay respect to another is the same as respecting yourself. The self and the other are ultimately inseparable.

This Question of Who We Are

Harding: When you talk about dialogue, I sense that you assume there is something that each of us has to offer to others – that we are connected to one another by our capacity to give, to receive, and to share. You recognize that all living creatures exist to feed and nurture one another, that we are here to be of value to one another, and that this is the way that we manifest the divine spirit. Indeed, this is the path that all the great teachers of humankind have shown us.

IKEDA: This relates closely to the story taught in the Lotus Sutra about the practice of Bodhisattva Never Disparaging, whom I discussed earlier (see Conversation Six). Bodhisattva Never Disparaging, again, persevered in his practice of veneration and respect for all people. In his teachings, Nichiren used the example of Bodhisattva Never Disparaging to explain that every person possesses the Buddha nature:

> 'Self' and 'others' are in fact not two different things. For this reason, when the bodhisattva Never Disparaging makes his bow of obeisance to the four kinds of believers, the Buddha nature inherent in the four kinds of believers of overbearing arrogance is bowing in obeisance to the bodhisattva Never Disparaging. It is like the situation when one faces a mirror and makes a bow of obeisance: the image in the mirror likewise makes a bow of obeisance to oneself.[6]

Acknowledging the dignity and worth, the Buddha nature, of the other, Bodhisattva Never Disparaging persevered in dialogue. In steadfastly carrying out this practice, he embodied life in all its nobility and dignity.

Profound respect for others is both the point at which all dialogue begins as well as its ultimate objective. With this belief in my heart, I have challenged myself to engage others in dialogue that transcends culture, religion and ideology.

In this age of globalization, we must become more cognizant

not only that we are connected to one another as part of humanity but that we are inextricably embedded in the ecological systems of nature and the Earth.

HARDING: In this regard, I was troubled by the April 2010 oil spill that occurred in the Gulf of Mexico.

My dear brother and friend, as you are well aware, we must recognize that peace in the human community is tied to our making peace with the natural world. Just as we, as human beings, must learn to appreciate one another, we must also develop a deeper recognition of our connections to the natural world, even to the world existing thousands of feet below the surface of the ocean.

More than half a century ago, Rachel Carson, a pioneer of the environmental movement, tried to lead us in the right direction. She warned that if we neglect our connection to the non-human world, we will never achieve our potential as human beings. We human beings cannot become fully human in isolation from other living beings. In all our endeavours, we should be joining hands with others rather than trying to dominate them. We should be learning from others as much as trying to teach others. I want to see us becoming more compassionate human beings and more consciously connected to the planet that we are an integral part of.

IKEDA: As Rachel Carson repeatedly stressed, human existence occupies a minute part of the vastness of the Earth and the universe. Recognizing that the Earth does not exist solely for our own purposes, we must seek to coexist with the natural world in a spirit of gratitude and awe for the magnificence of the workings of the universe.

Nichiren wrote: 'Without the body, no shadow can exist, and without life, no environment. In the same way, life is shaped by its environment.'[7] This teaching emphasizes that human beings and the environment (including nature and society) exist in a relationship of mutual influence. Human beings cannot exist without nature. Destroying the environment is the same as annihilating ourselves.

As Dr King pointed out, if we fail to maintain an attitude of reverence and humility toward nature, humankind will inevitably proceed down the path to self-destruction, brought on by our arrogant egotism and greed. Henceforth, the important mission of communities will be to cultivate an ethos of coexistence and convey this to the next generation.

HARDING: When we think of building a global community, we must consider what exactly the concept of community means. An essential aspect of this is to thoroughly know ourselves. Without this understanding of the self, there is a temptation to imitate, become totally dependent on, or completely reject the other. Consequently, creating a community becomes impossible.

To build a global community, we must earnestly seek answers to the questions of who we are and where we have come from. At present, globalization is perceived in terms of the materialistic dimension. This tends to lead to comparisons between ourselves and others based on how distinctive or how much better we think we are. If we want to develop a sense of global citizenship, we must go deeper into this question of who we are and recognize that at a fundamental level, we are indeed connected to every other being.

If the educational process of every child included a dimension of exploring another, unfamiliar part of the world, then we could start building this sense of global citizenship we are talking about. Just as we seek to fulfil our duty as citizens of our country, we must come to think of ourselves as citizens of the world, the Earth and the planet, and begin to ask what our role should be. What is the task that we must fulfil? This approach will give us a different perspective on the world.

The Courage To Dream

Ikeda: Indeed, we are connected to every other being on Earth. This thought relates, again, to the Buddhist concept of dependent origination, which views all phenomena in the universe as interdependent. Phenomena do not exist in isolation; everything in the world arises and comes into existence through relationships with other phenomena.

Self and other, the individual and society, human beings and nature, human beings and the planet Earth, humanity and the universe – all these dichotomies arise and develop in a dynamic relationship of mutual influence and interaction. Pursuing and committing to a way of life based on the harmonious coexistence recognized in this view of humanity, the world and the universe fosters global citizenship.

In a talk titled 'Thoughts on Education for Global Citizenship' delivered at Columbia University Teachers College in 1996, I pointed out the following three essential qualities that I think every global citizen should possess:

> (1) the wisdom to perceive the interconnectedness of all life and living [beings]; (2) the courage not to fear or deny difference, but to respect and strive to understand people of different cultures, and to grow from encounters with them; (3) the compassion to maintain an imaginative empathy that reaches beyond one's immediate surroundings and extends to those suffering in distant places.[8]

Harding: The three qualities for global citizenship that you mentioned are imperative. Of the three, courage is at the heart of so much because, as Walt Whitman and Langston Hughes have pointed out, we need courage to be willing to dream. It takes courage to put yourself into that which does not yet exist – to step out and to let that dream possess you, and then to act on it. So, courage is involved in every part of the process.

IKEDA: Without courage, nothing happens. Indeed, courage is the primary requirement for the expression of wisdom and compassion.

This is a point that Josei Toda often stressed when talking to the youth on the importance of having courage in the pursuit of justice. He said:

> As ordinary mortals, it can sometimes be difficult for us to summon forth compassion, but we can substitute courage for compassion. The courage to speak the truth is equivalent to compassion.[9]

If you were to identify people in the United States who could be called global citizens, whom would you name?

HARDING: I have already mentioned a number of true leaders among the people. If we follow the conventional definition of leadership, I would say that President Obama has the most potential to become a great leader. Compared to other leaders, I feel that this president is so much more insightful about people. Yet it seems that he is having difficulty knowing how to manifest this power.

One characteristic that we seek in a president, which is illustrated in King's life, is the moral fortitude to follow his or her insights about what is necessary for the welfare of the country and the people. And so, for the sake of uplifting American democracy, we want to encourage courageous leadership in facing the challenges of racism/white supremacy, materialism and militarism.

IKEDA: I sense your high hopes for President Obama. We must have courage inspired by a steadfast, determined personal faith.

Without this resolve, we will be unable to achieve any meaningful change.

W. E. B. Du Bois, another American leader for human rights, rallied the people with this clarion call: 'The morning breaks over the hills. Courage, brothers! The battle for humanity is not lost or losing.'[10]

Dr Du Bois played a leading role in organizing the Pan-African movement and devoted himself to working for African independence. For the past fifty years, I have maintained that the twenty-first century will be the Century of Africa. My sincere desire all along has been to see Africa's advancement and the African people's progress. Are there any African leaders whom you hold in high regard?

HARDING: Africa today is made up of more than fifty countries. Each of these experiences similar difficulties and hopes, but each is a small part of a massive continent. We must not forget that each has its distinctive identity.

Among the countries of Africa, South Africa is unique. A quarter of a century ago, most people expected that apartheid would not end without terrible bloodshed. Yet a national catastrophe was averted, and a peaceful transition was made to a more equitable social and governmental system. South Africa is now learning how to be a multiracial democracy. I am sure that this process will not be completely painless, but I am hopeful.

In my opinion, Nelson Mandela, South Africa's first post-apartheid president and the one who brought about radical reform, was a courageous leader who fought against brutal adversaries for the sake of the next generation of South Africans not even been born yet.

IKEDA: I have had the opportunity to meet twice with Nelson Mandela in Tokyo. The first time was in 1990, the year that Mr

Mandela was released from prison, and the second time was in 1995, when he visited Japan in his official capacity as South Africa president. The beaming smile of this fearless champion of human rights left a powerful impression on me.

President Mandela was imprisoned for ten thousand days. In spite of being incarcerated for such a long period – totalling twenty-seven and a half years – he proved that he was indeed a great man and preeminent global citizen. The struggle of Mr Mandela and his colleagues to crush the system of apartheid was a battle to defend humanity and forge a path to an unexplored frontier in human history.

Indeed, as you point out, President Mandela's struggle was waged on behalf of children not yet born. Global citizens live their lives not only for the present but for the distant future. They are concerned about subsequent generations of leaders. During his visits to Japan, President Mandela seemed to be thrilled by his interactions with our young people, including students from Soka University.

Speaking of Soka University, I am reminded that your son, Jonathan, spent some time studying at Soka University in Tokyo. As university founder, I am happy that we could host him, as I trust he has good memories of his time there.

HARDING: My son told me that he always felt welcomed, just as I have, by everyone at Soka University. When a student feels safe and valued in a learning environment, he or she can have a much more productive learning experience.

IKEDA: I was told that your son is a pleasant young man, well-liked by his peers. Please convey my best regards to him. Soka University is his alma mater, so please let him know that he is welcome anytime.

You have visited our campuses in Japan and the United States, providing stimulating, enlightening experiences for our students. For this, I cannot thank you enough.

We were pleased that in a 2010 *Newsweek* ranking of US colleges and universities, Soka University of America, which has been in existence for a mere ten years, ranked high in four categories. For example, in the '25 Most Diverse Schools', a category based on students' ethnicity and place of origin, it placed twelfth, after such prestigious schools as the University of Pennsylvania and the Massachusetts Institute of Technology.

Seekers

Harding: I am grateful that Soka University of America has spoken out and demonstrated that it is an educational institution that encourages students to dedicate themselves to the cause of peace and a more just and democratic world. Having such a diverse student body is a significant and invaluable advantage. The university should build on this diversity and let the stories and experiences of the students become a major component of the teaching resources of the institution.

Wherever I go, I ceaselessly pose the question, 'What kind of education will prepare people – especially young people – to become active, engaged citizens in a multiracial democratic society?' The answer can be found in the exemplary model of education offered by Soka University of America.

Ikeda: Thank you so much. As articulated in our school motto, SUA students strive to 'be philosophers of a renaissance of life; be world citizens in solidarity for peace; be the pioneers of a global civilization'.[11] This university was founded to cultivate leaders who will contribute to the creation of a harmonious human community in the twenty-first, twenty-second, twenty-third centuries and beyond. Inspired by these principles, talented young people from all over the world have enthusiastically gathered at the university.

If the main objective for SUA students was to simply receive educational credentials in order to obtain jobs, they probably could have chosen a more established university. However, our students have embraced their mission to wage a struggle as pioneers to create a new chapter in human history. To this end, they have dedicated themselves to personal elevation and self-improvement through learning while developing and building their university. I am absolutely committed to giving them my complete support.

HARDING: This is magnificent because it is so unusual in the world of higher education. It's important to keep reminding students that the jobs that are available today may not have much relevance five or ten years from now. Therefore, they need to be preparing themselves not for a particular job slot that exists today; they should be striving to become more creative so that they can open up new, yet to be conceived avenues of creative work for themselves.

IKEDA: At Soka University of America, our hope is to nurture global citizens who will spread their wings and fly. We want them to become leaders who have a sincere commitment to serving the people, who courageously act for the cause of peace and justice and who wisely honour and protect the global environment and the biological and social diversity of life on Earth.

In the short span of our university's history, we have hosted – in addition to many distinguished American scholars and leaders, yourself included – the Nobel Peace Prize laureates Sir Joseph Rotblat and Ms Betty Williams from the United Kingdom. These experiences have been invaluable and inspiring for our students.

HARDING: Each time I visit Soka University of America, I come away inspired. I remember that I especially felt this way after my most recent visit.

If I were to articulate the reason for my appreciation of Soka University of America, I would have to say that I see it as a place of hope. It is a place where, at your invitation, young people from all over the world gather to discover their purpose in life. They come not simply to get what we call 'an education' and certainly not just, as you say, to receive educational credentials. They come to be challenged to discover themselves as world citizens and as leaders whose ultimate purpose is to recreate their societies and their world.

A friend and I once led a seminar at Soka University of America that focused on the world-famous movie *Avatar*. The heart of the discussion revolved around the overarching question, 'What is human nature?' I found the students ready to grapple with and reflect on this question. Their openness to that kind of inquiry impressed me.

I am reminded of the old Quaker term, which I really like, that describes religious faith as *an act of seekers*. In my experience, there are many wonderful seekers at Soka University of America.

IKEDA: *Seekers* – what a profoundly moving expression. I would say that the global citizens that we hope to nurture are eternal seekers engaged in a search for truths about human existence, life and the universe. They are eternal advocates for justice, battling to triumph over injustice. They are eternal activists whose goal is to rid the world of human misery and enable all people to enjoy their right to happiness. The dream of a better world embraced by Dr King and shared by both of us will surely be realized by this younger generation, which has accepted its mission as global citizens. This is why I am determined that, with 'We Shall Overcome' ringing in our hearts, we must continue to do our utmost to open up opportunities for young people to take their place as the leaders of tomorrow.

Harding: Yes, my brother, perhaps together we could speak to our young people in words that I have recently come across from Canadian educator Claude Thomas Bissell – words that would be a good message from us to them: 'Risk more than others think is safe. Care more than others think is wise. Dream more than others think is practical. Expect more than others think is possible.'

APPENDIX 1

Selected Works

Daisaku Ikeda

Before It Is Too Late: A Dialogue, with Aurelio Peccei. London: I.B.Tauris & Co. Ltd, 2009 (first published in 1984).

Choose Life, with Arnold J. Toynbee. London: Oxford University Press, 1989.

Creating Waldens: An East–West Conversation on the American Renaissance, with Ronald A. Bosco and Joel Myerson. Cambridge: Dialogue Path Press, 2009.

Discussions on Youth. Santa Monica, CA: World Tribune Press, 2010.

The Human Revolution. Santa Monica, CA: World Tribune Press, 2004 (book 1 and book 2).

Into Full Flower: Making Peace Cultures Happen, with Elise Boulding. Cambridge: Dialogue Path Press, 2010.

Moral Lessons of the Twentieth Century: Gorbachev and Ikeda on Buddhism and Communism, with Mikhail Gorbachev. London: I.B.Tauris & Co. Ltd, 2005.

A New Humanism: The University Addresses of Daisaku Ikeda. London: I.B.Tauris & Co. Ltd, 2010.

The New Human Revolution. Santa Monica, CA: World Tribune Press: vol. 1, 1995; vol. 2, 1995; vol. 3, 1996; vol. 4, 1996; vol. 5, 1997; vol. 6, 1998; vol. 7, 2002; vol. 8, 2002; vol. 9, 2003; vol. 10, 2004; vol. 11, 2005; vol. 12, 2006; vol. 13, 2007; vol. 14, 2007; vol. 15, 2008; vol. 16, 2008; vol. 17, 2009; vol. 18, 2009; vol. 19, 2009; vol. 20, 2010; vol. 21, 2010; vol. 22, 2010; vol. 23, 2013.

The Persistence of Religion: Comparative Perspectives on Modern Spirituality, with Harvey G. Cox. London: I.B.Tauris & Co. Ltd, 2009.

A Quest for Global Peace: Rotblat and Ikeda on War, Ethics and the Nuclear Threat, with Joseph Rotblat. London: I.B.Tauris & Co. Ltd, 2007.

For more information, go to <http://www.daisakuikeda.org/sub/books/books-by-category.html>.

APPENDIX 2

Selected Works

Vincent Harding

There Is a River: The Black Struggle for Freedom in America. New York: Harcourt Brace Jovanovich, 1981.

Hope and History: Why We Must Share the Story of the Movement. Maryknoll, NY: Orbis Books, 1990, 2009.

We Changed the World: African Americans 1945–1970 (The Young Oxford History of African Americans, vol. 9). New York: Oxford University Press, 1997.

Martin Luther King: The Inconvenient Hero. Maryknoll, NY: Orbis Books, 2008.

Notes

Preface By Daisaku Ikeda

1. The Soka Junior and Senior High Schools, established by Daisaku Ikeda in Kodaira, Tokyo, in 1968, were the beginning of the Soka schools system, which today includes kindergartens, elementary schools, junior and senior high schools, a university in Japan and a university in Aliso Viejo, California Kindergartens have also been established in Hong Kong, Singapore, Malaysia, South Korea and Brazil. The educational system is based on the pedagogy of founding Soka Gakkai president and educator Tsunesaburo Makiguchi, who believed that the focus of education should be the lifelong happiness of the learner. Makiguchi was concerned with the development of the unique personality of each child, and he emphasized the importance of leading a socially contributive life.
2. Martin Luther King Jr, *Where Do We Go From Here: Chaos or Community?*, with a new introduction by Vincent Harding (Boston: Beacon Press, 2010), pp. 193–94.

Preface By Vincent Harding

1. The National Council of Elders was founded by the Rev. James Lawson, Dr Vincent Harding and the Rev. Phil Lawson and comprises veterans of the civil rights movement, the feminist movement, the

environmental movement, the immigrant rights movement and the gay rights movement. The goal of its members is to continue their work in social justice and impart the wisdom of their experiences to a new generation of social justice activists. For more information, see <http://www.nationalcouncilofelders.com/index.html>.

2. The phrase 'more perfect Union' references the Preamble to the US Constitution: 'We the People of the United States, in Order to form a more perfect Union . . .'
3. Hurricane Sandy was a Category 3 storm that struck portions of the Caribbean and eastern United States in late October 2012. It became the largest Atlantic hurricane on record, with winds spanning 1,100 miles. Damage was estimated at nearly US$75 billion.
4. Remarks by President Barack Obama to a joint session of Congress on health care, 9 September 2009, US Capitol. See <http://www.whitehouse.gov/the_press_office/Remarks-by-the-President-to-a-Joint-Session-of-Congress-on-Health-Care>.

Conversation One
A More Perfect Union

1. This dialogue was originally serialized in Japanese in *Daisanbunmei*, a monthly magazine, from February 2010–May 2011 (Nos 602–17). Dr Harding and President Ikeda first met in Tokyo, January 1994.
2. Coretta Scott King, *The Words of Martin Luther King Jr.* (New York: Newmarket Press, 2008), p. 17.
3. (trans. from Japanese) *Mainichi Shimbun*, 24 February 2008.
4. T. Denean Sharpley-Whiting, ed., *The Speech: Race and Barack Obama's "A More Perfect Union"* (New York: Bloomsbury USA, 2009), p. 246.
5. The Preamble to the US Constitution reads in toto: 'We the People of the United States, in Order to form a more perfect Union, establish Justice, insure domestic Tranquility, provide for the common defence, promote the general Welfare, and secure the Blessings of Liberty to ourselves and our Posterity, do ordain and establish this Constitution for the United States of America.'
6. Sharpley-Whiting, ed., *The Speech*, p. 238.
7. Ibid.

8. Martin Luther King Jr, *Why We Can't Wait*, with a new introduction by Dorothy Cotton (Boston: Beacon Press, 2010), p. 87.
9. Vincent Harding, *Hope and History: Why We Must Share the Story of the Movement* (Maryknoll, NY: Orbis Books, 1990, 2009), pp. 190–203.
10. From the early 1930s through World War II, imperial Japan tried to unify the people with State Shinto as the spiritual backbone of wars it fought and the Peace Preservation Law of 1925 as the means for thought control. Charged with violation of the Peace Preservation Law, twenty-one leaders of the Soka Kyoiku Gakkai (Value-Creating Education Society) were arrested and imprisoned, beginning with Tsunesaburo Makiguchi, then president of the organization, and Josei Toda. Most of them abandoned their faith and renounced their association with Makiguchi and Toda. Makiguchi upheld his faith and died in prison in 1944. His disciple, Toda, was released on parole just before the end of the war and then embarked on the reconstruction of their lay movement, which he renamed Soka Gakkai (Value-Creation Society).
11. Martin Luther King Jr, 'Nobel Prize Acceptance Speech' in *A Testament of Hope: The Essential Writings and Speeches of Martin Luther King, Jr.*, James M. Washington, ed. (New York: HarperCollins, 1986), pp. 224–30.
12. Mikhail Gorbachev and Daisaku Ikeda, *Moral Lessons of the Twentieth Century: Gorbachev and Ikeda on Buddhism and Communism* (London: I.B.Tauris & Co. Ltd, 2005), p. 14.
13. The 2010 United States Census indicates that, while the white population increased between 2000 and 2010, it did so at a lower rate than the nation as a whole (see <http://www.census.gov/prod/cen2010/briefs/c2010br-05.pdf>). The Pew Research Centre reports that Hispanics account for more than half of the United States' growth in population from 2000 to 2010 (see <http://www.pewhispanic.org/2011/03/24/hispanics-account-for-more-than-half-of-nations-growth-in-past-decade/>).
14. The Immigration and Nationality Act of 1965 (Hart–Celler Act) marked a radical break from previous immigration policies. Until then, Asians and Africans were excluded, and immigration policies gave preference to northern and western Europeans over southern and eastern ones.

15. For more information, see 'Overview of Race and Hispanic Origin: 2010', part of the results of the 2010 United States Census, at <http://www.census.gov/prod/cen2010/briefs/c2010br-02.pdf>.
16. Walt Whitman, *Leaves of Grass* in *Poetry and Prose*, Justin Kaplan, ed. (New York: Library of America, 1982), p. 272.
17. Passed by the United States Congress on 31 January 1865, and ratified on 6 December 1865, the Thirteenth Amendment abolished slavery in the United States. It provides that 'Neither slavery nor involuntary servitude, except as a punishment for crime whereof the party shall have been duly convicted, shall exist within the United States, or any place subject to their jurisdiction.'
18. The Jim Crow laws refer to state and local laws enacted between 1876 and 1965 that mandated *de jure* racial segregation with, starting in 1890, a 'separate but equal' status for African Americans. They led in practice to conditions that tended to be inferior to those provided for whites. They also systematized a number of economic, educational and social disadvantages for African Americans.
19. King, 'A Christmas Sermon on Peace' in *A Testament of Hope*, p. 257.

Conversation Two
A Brilliant Test of Human Nature

1. Alexis de Tocqueville, *Democracy in America and Two Essays on America* (New York: Penguin Classics, 2003), p. 742.
2. Coretta Scott King, *The Words of Martin Luther King, Jr.*, p. 19.
3. Nichiren, *The Writings of Nichiren Daishonin*, vol. 1 (Tokyo: Soka Gakkai, 1999), p. 217.
4. (trans. from Japanese) Chang Shuhong and Daisaku Ikeda, *Tonko no kosai* (The Radiance of Dunhuang: On Beauty and Life) (Tokyo: Tokuma Shoten, 1990).
5. One of Daisaku Ikeda's first initiatives, five months after his 3 May 1960 inauguration as Soka Gakkai president, was to travel to the United States, Canada and Brazil to encourage the handful of Soka Gakkai members there. That marked the beginning of his global vision for peace based on Buddhist principles.
6. Langston Hughes, 'The Negroe Speaks of Rivers' in *The Collected Poems of Langston Hughes*, Arnold Rampersand and David Roessel, eds (New York: Vintage Classics, 1995), p. 23.

Conversation Three
The Coming of the New America

1. Thomas Hornsby Ferril, 'Here Is a Land Where Life Is Written in Water' in *Thomas Hornsby Ferril and the American West*, Robert C. Baron, Stephen J. Leonard, and Thomas J. Noel, eds (Golden, CO: Fulcrum, 1996), p. 36.
2. 'Strive with Unceasing Effort and Courage', message to the junior high and high school division graduation, 16 March 2003; Bonus Articles, *SGI-USA Publications 1997–2008* (CD).
3. Tsunesaburo Makiguchi, *A Geography of Human Life*, Dayle Bethel, trans. (San Francisco, CA: Caddo Gap Press, 2002), p. 62.
4. Whitman is quoted in Horace Traubel, *With Walt Whitman in Camden*, vol. 5, Gertrude Traubel, ed. (Carbondale, IL: Southern Illinois University Press, 1964), p. 357. See also the online Walt Whitman Archive, <http://whitmanarchive.org/criticism/disciples/traubel/WWWiC/5/med.00005.94.html>.
5. Ibid., p. 272.
6. Whitman, 'Spirit That Form'd This Scene' in *Poetry and Prose*, p. 594.
7. Maria Guajardo is an educator and community advocate. She has served on President Clinton's Minority Mental Health panel, which identified health care gaps and resources for the Latino community, and as executive director of the Mayor's Office for Education and Children in Denver, Colorado.
8. Founded in 1997 by Vincent and Rosemarie Freeney Harding, the Veterans of Hope Project 'is a multifaceted educational initiative on religion, culture and participatory democracy and encourages a healing-centreed approach to community building that recognizes the interconnectedness of spirit, creativity and citizenship'. See <http://www.veteransofhope.org>.
9. Adam Schrager, *The Principled Politician: The Ralph Carr Story* (Golden, CO: Fulcrum Publishing, 2008), p. 193. See also the Governor Ralph L. Carr Collection at the Colorado State Archives, <http://www.colorado.gov/dpa/doit/archives/govs/carr.html>.
10. King, *Where Do We Go From Here: Chaos or Community?*, p. 183.
11. Mrs Rosa Parks and President Ikeda first met on this occasion, 30 January 1993. She visited Soka University in Japan in 1994, when she received an honorary doctorate.

12. There are a number of theories that attempt to explain the connection, including: 1) good friends encourage their friends to lead healthier lifestyles; 2) good friends encourage their friends to seek help when needed; 3) good friends enhance their friends' coping skills in dealing with illness and other health problems; and 4) good friends actually affect physiological pathways that are protective of health. A ten-year Australian study published in the *Journal of Epidemiology and Community Health* (2005, Volume 59, Issue 7) found that older people with a large circle of friends were 22 per cent less likely to die during the study period than those with fewer friends.
13. In 2008, Harvard researchers reported that strong social ties could promote brain health as we age. In addition, not only does a happy friend mean we are more likely to be happy ourselves, it affects the larger social network. See David Cameron, 'Having Happy Friends Can Make You Happy', *Harvard Gazette*, 5 December 2008.
14. *The Book of the Kindred Sayings (Samyutta-Nikaya) or Grouped Suttas* (Oxford: The Pali Text Society, 1996), p. 113.

Conversation Four
Extraordinary Character

1. Maya Angelou interview conducted by the Academy of Achievement on 22 January 1997. For transcript and video, see <http://www.achievement.org/autodoc/page/angoint-1>.
2. Mohandas K. Gandhi, *All Men are Brothers: Autobiographical Reflections* (New York: Continuum, 2005), p. 166.
3. Daisaku Ikeda, *The Human Revolution*, book 1 (Santa Monica, CA: World Tribune Press, 2004), p. 807.
4. Mohandas K. Gandhi, 'The Doctrine of the Sword' in *Young India, Ahmedabad*, 11 August 1920.
5. King, 'Antidotes to Fear' in *A Testament of Hope*, p. 513.
6. Arnold Toynbee and Daisaku Ikeda, *Choose Life* (London: I.B.Tauris & Co. Ltd, 2007).
7. *The Lotus Sutra and Its Opening and Closing Sutras*, Burton Watson, trans. (Tokyo: Soka Gakkai, 2009), p. 56.
8. Ibid., p. 258.
9. President Lyndon Johnson manoeuvred legislation through Congress,

and on 2 July 1964, signed the Civil Rights Act of 1964, which banned discrimination based on 'race, color, religion, sex or national origin' in employment practices and public accommodations. The law also nullified state and local laws that required such discrimination.

Conversation Five
On Encouragement

1. Coretta Scott King, *The Words of Martin Luther King, Jr.*, p. 17.
2. See note 1 in Conversation One above.
3. Nichiren (1222–82) is the founder of the Buddhist tradition that is based on the Lotus Sutra and urges chanting the phrase *Nam-myoho-renge-kyo* as a daily practice. The Soka Gakkai International is based on Nichiren's teachings. (Source: *The Soka Gakkai Dictionary of Buddhism*, p. 439)
4. Nichiren, *The Writings of Nichiren Daishonin*, vol. 1, p. 1086.
5. Nichiren, *The Record of the Orally Transmitted Teachings* (Tokyo: Soka Gakkai, 2004), pp. 211–12.
6. *The Lotus Sutra and Its Opening and Closing Sutras*, p. 65.
7. Elise Boulding and Daisaku Ikeda, *Into Full Flower: Making Peace Cultures Happen* (Cambridge, MA: Dialogue Path Press, 2010).
8. Nichiren, *The Writings of Nichiren Daishonin*, vol. 1, p. 401.
9. Pete Daniel, *Lost Revolutions: The South in the 1950s* (Washington, DC: University of North Carolina Press for Smithsonian National Museum of American History, 2000), p. 291.
10. Joseph Rotblat and Daisaku Ikeda, *A Quest for Global Peace: Rotblat and Ikeda on War, Ethics, and the Nuclear Threat* (London: I.B.Tauris & Co. Ltd, 2007), p. 109.
11. Ibid., p. 108.
12. During the 1960s, the FBI's counterintelligence program (called 'COINTELPRO') infiltrated many activist social change groups it deemed as threats to the United States, including groups associated with Martin Luther King Jr, along with other anti-racism and anti-war organizations. The goal of infiltration was not just to gather intelligence but also to promote internal dissension and provoke disruptive activities that could publicly discredit the group being targeted. See Nelson Blackstock, *COINTELPRO: The FBI's Secret War on*

Political Freedom (New York: Pathfinder, 1975 [first published by Vintage Books, 1975]). See also Brian Glick, *War At Home: Covert Action Against U.S. Activists and What We Can Do About It* (Boston: South End Press, 1989).

Conversation Six
Influential Encounters

1. *The Autobiography of Martin Luther King, Jr.*, Clayborne Carson, ed. (New York: Grand Central Publishing, 2001), p. 6. This book was compiled after King's death by Carson, director of the Martin Luther King Jr Papers Project at Stanford University, from King's extant autobiographies, along with previously published and unpublished writings, interviews and speeches.
2. Ibid., p. 3.
3. Ibid., p. 4.
4. Adolfo Pérez Esquivel and Daisaku Ikeda, *Jinken no seiki e no messeji* (Message for the Age of Human Rights) (Tokyo: The Institute of Oriental Philosophy, 2009), p. 181.
5. *The Autobiography of Martin Luther King, Jr.*, p. 4.
6. Martin Luther King Jr, *Stride Toward Freedom: The Montgomery Story*, with a new introduction by Clayborne Carson (Boston: Beacon Press, 2010), p. 6.
7. *Walking Integrity: Benjamin Elijah Mays, Mentor to Martin Luther King Jr.*, Lawrence Edward Carter, Sr, ed. (Macon, GA: Mercer University Press, 1988), pp. 201–2.
8. Benjamin Elijah Mays, *Seeking to Be a Christian in Race Relations* (New York: Friendship Press, 1957).
9. Mohandas K. Gandhi, *The Collected Works of Mahatma Gandhi*, vol. 68 (New Delhi, India: The Publications Division, Ministry of Information and Broadcasting, Government of India, 1977), pp. 237–38.
10. King, *Stride Toward Freedom*, pp. 84–85.
11. Gandhi, *The Collected Works*, vol. 73, p. 148.
12. *The Lotus Sutra and Its Opening and Closing Sutras*, p. 308.
13. Nichiren, *The Writings of Nichiren Daishonin*, vol. 1, p. 287.
14. Ibid.

Conversation Seven
The Expansion of Democracy

1. Rosa Parks and Jim Haskins, *Rosa Parks: My Story* (New York: Puffin, 1999), p. 117.
2. *Quiet Strength: The Faith, the Hope, and the Heart of a Woman Who Changed a Nation,* Rosa L. Parks and Gregory J. Reed, eds (Grand Rapids, MI: Zondervan Publishing House, 1994), p. 23.
3. King, *Stride Toward Freedom*, p. 48.
4. 'Address to the First Montgomery Improvement Association Meeting' in *A Call to Conscience: The Landmark Speeches of Dr. Martin Luther King, Jr.*, Clayborne Carson and Kris Shepard, eds (New York: Warner Books, 2002), p. 10.
5. King, *Stride Toward Freedom*, p. xxx.
6. Ibid., pp. 63–64.
7. *A Call to Conscience,* p. 4.
8. *The Autobiography of Martin Luther King, Jr.*, p. 115.
9. King, *Stride Toward Freedom*, p. 138.
10. Ibid., p. 141.
11. Daisaku Ikeda, *The New Human Revolution*, vol. 3 (Santa Monica, CA: World Tribune Press, 1996), p. 92.
12. In 1957, a number of Soka Gakkai members were accused of violating the vote solicitation clause of the Election Law, and prosecutors charged Daisaku Ikeda as the responsible person. On 3 July 1957, he was arrested and jailed for two weeks. Prosecutors were armed with forced confessions from Soka Gakkai members and also pressured Daisaku Ikeda to sign a false confession, threatening to arrest Soka Gakkai President Josei Toda, who was in declining health. He refused, and it became clear that the arrest of Soka Gakkai members provided a pretext to attack the Soka Gakkai. The case dragged out in court for four and a half years, during which it was revealed that the prosecution had falsified the interrogation transcripts of the arrested Soka Gakkai members. Ikeda was finally exonerated of all charges in January 1962.
13. Rabindranath Tagore, *Stray Birds* (New York: The Macmillan Company, 1916), p. 89.

Conversation Eight
When Youth Took the Lead

1. The Freedom Rides were launched during the spring of 1961 by student activists from the Congress of Racial Equality. Freedom Riders initially travelled from Washington, DC, to Jacksonville, Mississippi. By the end of the summer, the Freedom Rides had spread to train stations and airports across the South, and in November, an Interstate Commerce Commission ruling prohibiting segregated transportation facilities took effect. See the website of Stanford University's Martin Luther King, Jr Research and Education Institute: <http://mlk-kpp01.stanford.edu/indcx.php/encyclopedia/encyclopedia/enc_freedom_rides/>.
2. King, 'The Time for Freedom Has Come' in *A Testament of Hope*, p. 162.
3. *The Autobiography of Martin Luther King, Jr.*, p. 37.
4. Nichiren, *The Writings of Nichiren Daishonin*, vol. 1, p. 656.
5. Kaneko Ikeda, *Kaneko's Story* (Santa Monica, CA: World Tribune Press, 2008), p. 38.

Conversation Nine
The Pivotal Struggle in Birmingham

1. Langston Hughes, 'Walkers with the Dawn' in *The Collected Poems*, p. 45.
2. Brown vs Board of Education, 347 US 483 (1954), was a landmark case in which the court declared state laws establishing separate public schools for black and white students unconstitutional. This ruling paved the way for integration and was a major victory of the civil rights movement.
3. King, *Why We Can't Wait*, p. 55.
4. Ibid., p. 67.
5. King, 'Letter from Birmingham Jail' in *Why We Can't Wait*, pp. 85–109. For an annotated version of the letter, see the website of Stanford University's Martin Luther King, Jr, Research and Education Institute: <http://mlk-kpp01.stanford.edu/index.php/resources/article/annotated_letter_from_birmingham/>.

6. For the 'Statement by Alabama Clergyman', see the website of Stanford University's Martin Luther King, Jr Research and Education Institute: <http://mlk-kpp01.stanford.edu/kingweb/popular_requests/frequentdocs/clergy.pdf>.
7. Ibid.
8. Ibid.
9. King, *Why We Can't Wait*, p. 97.
10. Ibid, pp. 86, 87.
11. Ibid., p. 109.
12. Ibid., p. 112.
13. Richard D. Heffner, *A Documentary History of the United States* (New York: Signet Classic, 2002), pp. 399–400.

Conversation Ten
The March on Washington

1. King, *Why We Can't Wait*, p. 131.
2. Ibid., pp. 137–38.
3. Ibid., p. 144.
4. *The Autobiography of Martin Luther King, Jr.*, p. 222.
5. King, 'I Have a Dream' in *A Testament of Hope*, p. 218
6. Ibid., p. 219
7. King, 'A Christmas Sermon on Peace' in *A Testament of Hope*, p. 257.
8. King, 'I Have a Dream' in *A Testament of Hope*, p. 219.
9. Nichiren, *The Writings of Nichiren Daishonin*, vol. 1, p. 279.
10. King, 'Eulogy for the Martyred Children' in *A Testament of Hope*, p. 222.
11. Ibid.
12. Ibid.
13. On 20 September 2008, the Ikeda Centre for Peace, Learning and Dialogue in Cambridge, Massachusetts, held its fifth annual Ikeda Forum for Intercultural Dialogue to explore how fearlessly facing death can produce significant personal and social benefits. Titled 'Living with Mortality: How Our Experiences With Death Change Us', the forum featured distinguished speakers Pam Kircher, Anthony Marsella, Megan Laverty and Vincent Harding.
14. Daisaku Ikeda, 'Mahayana Buddhism and Twenty-first-Century

Civilization' in *A New Humanism: The University Addresses of Daisaku Ikeda* (London and New York: I.B.Tauris & Co. Ltd, 2010), pp. 165–75.

15. In Buddhism, Nichiren divides life's 'treasures' into three categories: treasures of the storehouse, treasures of the body and treasures of the heart. He wrote: 'More valuable than treasures in a storehouse are treasures of the body, and the treasures of the heart are the most valuable of all. Strive to accumulate the treasures of the heart!' (*The Writings of Nichiren Daishonin*, vol. 1, p. 1170).
16. King, 'Nobel Prize Acceptance Speech' in *A Testament of Hope*, p. 225.
17. Ibid.

Conversation Eleven
Beyond Vietnam

1. Ikeda, *The Human Revolution*, book 1, p. 3.
2. King, 'A Time to Break Silence' in *A Testament of Hope*, p. 235.
3. King, 'Remaining Awake Through a Great Revolution' in *A Testament of Hope*, pp. 276–77.
4. King, 'A Time to Break Silence' in *A Testament of Hope*, p. 231.
5. Jeannette Rankin (11 June 1880–18 May 1973) was the first woman in the United States Congress. She was first elected to represent Montana in 1916 and again in 1940. A lifelong pacifist, she was one of fifty members of Congress to vote against entry into World War I in 1917. In 1941, she was the only member of Congress to vote against declaring war on Japan after its attack on Pearl Harbor on 7 December 1941.
6. Gandhi, *All Men Are Brothers*, p. 168.
7. Ikeda, *The New Human Revolution*, vol. 6 (Santa Monica, CA: World Tribune Press, 1998), pp. 46–47.
8. The Vietnam War resulted in the deaths of 195,000–430,000 South Vietnamese civilians, 50,000–65,000 North Vietnamese civilians, 171,331–220,357 soldiers from the Army of the Republic of Vietnam, probably somewhere near 444,000 communist forces and 58,220 US service members. The most detailed demographic study calculated 791,000–1,141,000 war-related deaths for all of Vietnam. The effects of the war of US service members is thought to be a major factor in the high rate of suicide in the following years (approximately

60,000). From Guenter Lewy, *America in Vietnam* (New York: Oxford University Press, 1978), pp. 450–53; also from Thomas C. Thayer, *War Without Fronts: The American Experience in Vietnam* (Boulder, CO: Westview Press, 1985), chap. 12.

Conversation Twelve
A Revolution of Values

1. *The Autobiography of Martin Luther King, Jr*, p. 342.
2. The day after King's 'I Have a Dream' speech in August 1963, FBI Intelligence Chief William Sullivan authored a report in which he said: 'In the light of King's powerful demagogic speech … We must mark him now, if we have not done so before, as the most dangerous Negro of the future in this Nation from the standpoint of communism, the Negro and national security.' From Tim Weiner, *Enemies: A History of the FBI* (New York: Random House Digital, Inc., 2012), p. 245.
3. Ronald A. Bosco, Joel Myerson and Daisaku Ikeda, *Creating Waldens: An East–West Conversation on the American Renaissance* (Cambridge, MA: Dialogue Path Press, 2009), pp. 16–17.
4. King, 'A Time to Break Silence' in *A Testament of Hope*, p. 240.
5. Ibid.
6. Ibid.
7. From Abraham Lincoln's inaugural address, given on 4 March 1861: 'the better angels of our nature'.
8. Poor People's Campaign: Conceived by Martin Luther King Jr and carried out in the wake of his assassination, the campaign demanded economic and human rights for poor blacks, Chicanos, Indians and whites, based on the understanding that people should have what they need to live.
9. Nichiren, *The Writings*, vol. 1, p. 851.
10. King, 'A Time to Break Silence' in *A Testament of Hope*, p. 242.

Conversation Thirteen
Non-violent Acts of Courage

1. King, 'Remaining Awake Through a Great Revolution' in *A Testament of Hope*, p. 275.

2. Ibid., p. 276.
3. Ibid.
4. Mohandas K. Gandhi, *An Autobiography: The Story of My Experiments with Truth*, Mahadev Desai, trans. (Boston: Beacon Press, 1957, 1993), p. xxvi.
5. King, 'The Trumpet of Conscience' in *A Testament of Hope*, p. 638.
6. Mohandas K. Gandhi, *The Words of Gandhi*, Richard Attenborough, ed. (New York: Newmarket Press, 2008), p. 89.
7. See the UNESCO website for the entire text: <http://www.unesco.org/new/en/unesco/about-us/who-we-are/history/constitution/>.
8. Nichiren, *The Writings of Nichiren Daishonin*, vol. 1, p. 989.
9. Rotblat and Ikeda, *A Quest for Global Peace*, p. 116.
10. Howard Thurman, *Disciplines of the Spirit* (Richmond, IN: Friends United Press, 1963), p. 45.
11. *The Gandhi Reader: A Sourcebook of His Life and Writings*, Homer A. Jack, ed. (New York: Grove Press, 1994), p. 315.

Conversation Fourteen
Carrying the Legacy Forward

1. Dr King was born on 15 January 1929.
2. King, *Stride Toward Freedom*, p. 190.
3. Nichiren, *The Record of the Orally Transmitted Teachings*, p. 115.
4. Nichiren, *The Writings of Nichiren Daishonin*, vol. 1, p. 1119.
5. King, *Where Do We Go from Here: Chaos or Community?*, p. 191.
6. Mahatma Gandhi, *The Essential Writings*, Judith M. Brown, ed. (Oxford: Oxford World Classics, 2008), p. 90.
7. Makiguchi, *A Geography of Human Life*, p. 286.
8. King, *Where Do We Go from Here: Chaos or Community?*, p. 196.
9. See Aurelio Peccei and Daisaku Ikeda, *Before It Is Too Late: A Dialogue* (London: I.B. Tauris & Co. Ltd, 1985).
10. Eknath Easwaran, *Gandhi the Man* (Petaluma, CA: Nilgiri Press, 1981), p. 11.
11. Nichiren, *The Writings of Nichiren Daishonin*, vol. 1, p. 385.
12. Ibid., p. 464.
13. Mohandas K. Gandhi, *All Men Are Brothers*, p. 162.
14. Ibid.

Conversation Fifteen
Start With a Dream

1. Traubel, *With Walt Whitman in Camden*, vol. 6, p. 139.
2. King, 'I Have a Dream' in *A Testament of Hope*, p. 219.
3. Daisaku Ikeda, *Discussions on Youth* (Santa Monica, CA: World Tribune Press, 2010), pp. 21–22.
4. Whitman, *Democratic Vistas* in *Poetry and Prose*, pp. 952, 959.
5. Hughes, 'Let America Be America Again' in *The Collected Poems*, p. 191.
6. Ibid., p. 189.
7. Hughes, 'Youth' in *The Collected Poems*, p. 39.
8. Daisaku Ikeda, *The Human Revolution*, book 2 (Santa Monica, CA: World Tribune Press, 2004), p. 1236.
9. Bloody Sunday, 7 March 1965: The first of three marches from Selma to Montgomery, Alabama, ended when 600 marchers – peacefully protesting the death of Jimmie Lee Jackson and the ongoing exclusion of blacks from the electoral process – were attacked by state and local police with billy clubs and tear gas. The second march on the following Tuesday resulted in 2,500 protesters turning around after crossing the Edmund Pettus Bridge. The third march started on 16 March. Marchers averaged ten miles a day and were protected by 2,000 US Army soldiers, 1,900 members of the Alabama National Guard, and many FBI agents and federal marshals. This third group reached its destination – the Alabama capitol in Montgomery – on 25 March. See the website of Stanford University's Martin Luther King, Jr Research and Education Institute: <http://mlk-kpp01.stanford.edu/index.php/encyclopedia/encyclopedia/enc_selma_to_montgomery_march/>.
10. Every year beginning in 1983, President Daisaku Ikeda has published a peace proposal on 26 January and submitted it to the United Nations. The 2011 peace proposal is available at <http://www.daisakuikeda.org/assets/files/peace2011.pdf>.
11. In his 2011 peace proposal, President Ikeda quoted Dr Harding: 'If, instead of referring to the movement as the "civil rights movement", we spoke in terms of "the expansion of democracy", then each new generation would recognize that they have a responsibility to expand

democracy beyond the way they found it. This duty is an ongoing task that each new generation must accept.' Translated from *Kibō no kyoiku, heiwa no koshin* [*Education of Hope, March of Peace*] (Tokyo: Daisanbunmei, August 2010), pp. 53–54.

12. Rabbi Abraham J. Heschel, 'The Religious Basis of Equality of Opportunity – The Segregation of God' in *Race: Challenge to Religion*, Mathew Ahmann, ed. (Chicago: Regnery, 1963), p. 69.
13. Nelson Mandela, in an interview with John Battersby in Johannesburg, South Africa, and published in *The Christian Science Monitor*, 10 February 2000. In Nelson Mandela, *Notes to the Future: Words of Wisdom* (New York: Atria Books, 2012), p. 83.
14. Whitman, *Democratic Vistas* in *Poetry and Prose*, p. 935.
15. Ibid., pp. 979–80.
16. Hughes, 'Dreams' in *The Collected Poems*, p. 32.

Conversation Sixteen
Becoming World Citizens

1. King, 'Remaining Awake Through a Great Revolution' in *A Testament of Hope*, p. 269.
2. Ibid.
3. Arnold Toynbee and Daisaku Ikeda, *Choose Life* (London: I.B.Tauris & Co. Ltd, 2007), p. 342.
4. King, 'Remaining Awake Through a Great Revolution' in *A Testament of Hope*, p. 269.
5. Ibid., p. 270.
6. Nichiren, *The Record of the Orally Transmitted Teachings*, p.165.
7. Nichiren, *The Writings of Nichiren Daishonin*, vol. 1, p. 644.
8. Daisaku Ikeda, 'Thoughts on Education for Global Citizenship' in *A New Humanism*, p. 55.
9. Daisaku Ikeda, 'Imparting Joy to Others', *World Tribune* (Santa Monica, CA: SGI-USA, 13 November 2009), p. 5.
10. John Henrik Clarke, *Black Titan: W. E. B. Du Bois* (Boston: Beacon Press, 1970), p. 21.
11. See the Soka University of America website, <http://www.soka.edu/about_soka/mission_and_values.aspx>.

Index